Scotland's Hidden Gems: Golf Courses and Pubs

By
Bob Jones

Pen & Print
139 NW 6th Ave.
Canby, Oregon 97013
USA

www.penandprint.com

Scotland's Hidden Gems:
Golf Courses and Pubs

Pen & Print
139 NW 6th Ave.
Canby, Oregon 97013 USA
www.penandprint.com

International Standard Book Number: 0-9765672-0-2

Design and page layout by
Michael Comfort
Vineyard Graphics, Inc.
www.vinegraphics.com

Table of Contents

FOREWORD by Rob Gibbons, PGA 1

INTRODUCTION: A Beginning 3

CHAPTER 1:   SOME QUESTIONS and a Few
Answers 5

CHAPTER 2:   THINGS YOU NEED TO KNOW
about Scottish Golf, Pubs, Driving,
and Touring 9

CHAPTER 3:   CENTRAL SCOTLAND around
Crieff 25

CHAPTER 4:   THE HIGHLAND ROAD: Up the A9
to Dornoch and North 49

CHAPTER 5:   THE NORTHEAST COAST 73

CHAPTER 6:   THE FIFE 91

CHAPTER 7:   THE BOARDERS and EAST
LOTHIANS around Peebles 111

CHAPTER 8:   SOUTHERN SCOTLAND along the
Solway Firth 131

CHAPTER 9:   AYR, ISLE ARRAN, and KINTYRE 145

CHAPTER 10:   THE BEST OF SCOTLAND 171

INDEX: 193

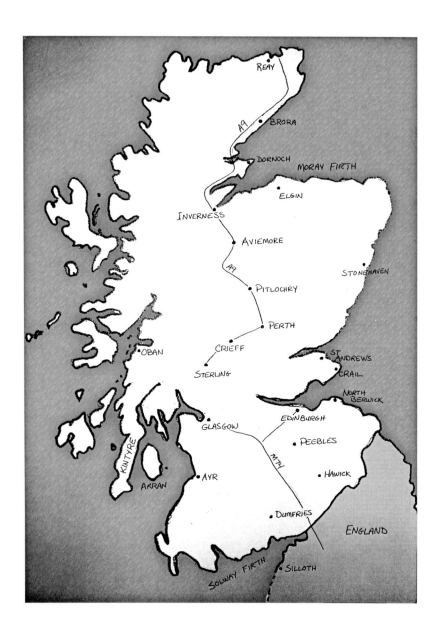

Foreword

by Rob Gibbons, PGA

As Head Golf Professional at Arrowhead Golf Club in Molalla, Oregon, I have traveled to Scotland three different times to enjoy the golf, the people, and the country. I have never been disappointed with any of my golf outings to Scotland, but I've never enjoyed the numerous golf courses or travel adventures that Bob and Anne Jones describe in *Scotland's Hidden Gems: Golf Courses and Pubs.*

All of my time in Scotland has been spent guiding golfers and playing courses of the British Open rotation. The trips have been wonderful experiences and I've loved every minute of them, but I now know that I have missed a big part of the Scotland golfing experience by not going to out-of-the-way courses, towns, and pubs while there. My next trip to Scotland will not be taken without this book. If you really want to see the country, play the courses that Scots play, know where the locals like to eat, stay in nice B&Bs and small guest houses that make you feel at home, and get a real feel for how friendly the people are...I believe this book is for you. It will help make your trip more complete whether you golf everyday or just prefer to drive the countryside.

Scotland's Hidden Gems is one of the only golf travel books that I've read which kept my interest throughout. It is an easy read and explores so many quaint towns and villages, as well as pubs and other eating establishments. As the authors point out visitor attractions and little-known golf courses, they also give travel tips, driving instructions, and information to help readers enjoy their golfing in Scotland. Best of all, the reader can enjoy the descriptions of the Joneses' golfing trips.

I will recommend this book to all who plan to visit Scotland.

Introduction:
A Beginning

In Fort Augustus, Scotland, we stop at the Tourist Information Bureau, "The I" of Scotland we term it, to make reservations for a few days ahead in yet another town. The girl behind the desk knows just the place for us in Crieff. "It's the best place in all Perthshire," she exclaims, "and it's got the awards to show it." She lets us know it will take at least an hour to confirm our lodging and suggests a place we might want to "...have a wee bite of lunch."

Thanking her, and wishing her luck at getting us a bed in the best of Perthshire, we take our leave and head for lunch in the direction she indicated. Our first query after leaving "The I" was to ask each other, "Perthshire?" A quick stop at the car retrieves the map which shows Perthshire. "Sterling to Perth," says Anne with a little authority, after all, she's been map reader now for almost 1500 miles. We both hope the Tourist Bureau girl reserves it for us.

After throwing the map back into the car, we strike out on foot toward our lunch goal, a place called something like the Loch Inn. Before we go half a block we make two discoveries. First, a tour bus lets out in the parking lot in front of us. Hordes of tourists—well, at least a dozen or two—hustle out of the bus and rush over, cameras clicking and whirring, to a bridge ahead of us. Second, we discover the reason for the shutterbugging: The bridge crosses the Caledonian Lock. As we work our way to the bridge, my camera clicking, we see several medium sized pleasure craft working their ways down the lock.

And there across from us is our objective, The Lock Inn and Gilliegorm Restaurant. The Inn turns out to be a positively quaint pub with an enticing selection of single malts, ales on tap, interesting soup specials, and a friendly barkeep who allows me to shoot a couple of interior photos, including one of him wiping a glass. Trite, maybe, but quaint.

The walk back to "The I" to check about our Perthshire lodging yields a pair of surprises. The first is just across the Lock from our lunch pub—a small museum dedicated to the history of the Caledonian Lock System. Even a ten minute stroll through the museum provides an informative background on the project. The second event is one of those easily missed or overlooked happenings that you might never know you missed until later and, then be all the sadder for it. As Anne

3

and I approach the Tourist Bureau office, I spy a dog in a stone-fenced and iron-gated yard across the road. Though I consider myself a "dog person" (having raced sled dogs for twelve years might have something to do with that), what attracts my attention is the red ball in the mouth of the black and white Aussie standing at the gate. As a pedestrian walks close to the gate, the Aussie tips her head (so coyly I was sure it was a she) and drops the ball so it bounced outside the gate in front of the approaching person, perhaps a tourist from the bus still parked in the lot. He looks first at the dog, then at the ball which had rolled in front of him, then picks up the ball and throws it back over the gate, and continus his walk. The dog chases the ball, grabs it, mauls it a little, then scampers back to the gate, ball in mouth, and waits for the next walker who could be enticed into throwing the ball for her. Clever, these Scottish-Aussie dogs!

Back at "The I," the girl greets us all smiles. "I've got great news. You're booked into Merlindale in Crieff. It was awarded Best B&B."

This hour-and-a-half visit to Fort Augustus was so typical of our six trips to Scotland over the past five years. Surprise, discovery, friendliness, history, beauty, and more surprises. As we immersed ourselves in the culture, Anne and I fell in love with Scotland. We both know we must have Scottish blood in our backgrounds—why else would we feel so comfortable, so at home, so connected!

It was early in our first visit in September, 2000, that we started to feel the connection. We had just finished playing golf at West Linton Golf Club, a nice 1890 built tract set in the middle of the Border's countryside, and were sitting in the Golden Arms Pub sipping a Coke and sharing a bag of chips with a golden retriever and a Heinz 57 pub mutt. The piano next to us had a note on it which read: "I like to be played. Please feel free." We gave each other that look that after thirty-five years of marriage says, "You're thinking the same thing, aren't you." I said, "Wouldn't it be fun to write about this...the golf...the pubs?" And Anne replied, "You do the writing, and I'll help with the research."

From that kernel of an idea, and after several trips to Scotland with golf every chance we could, eating in pubs for most meals, this book was born. *Scotland's Hidden Gems: Golf Courses and Pubs* was researched by two newly retired teachers and golfing duffers making their first excursions in international travel.

Chapter One:
Some Questions
and a Few Answers

If this is a book of information, questions must be asked and answers must be sought. The questions come easily, but the answers are sometimes harder to find. Let me try to answer some of the most important queries.

First, **why the connection between golf and pubs?** Besides the simple fact that both Anne and I enjoy golf and food and drink, there are some deeper connections. Both golf and pubs create their own cultures and those cultures overlap. Golfers, since the first shepherd hit a rock with a crooked stick into a rabbit hole, have wanted to "share" their good shots and their tragedies with anyone who would listen (and many who could care less). And what better place to share than over a pint or a dram (or both) at the neighborhood watering hole, the pub. Besides, after spending up to three and a half hours making a fool of yourself on the links, fighting gorse and gentle Scottish breezes (right!), many golfers find they need a pint to drown their sorrows or a dram to warm up their bones...or both!

Second, **why did we choose to concentrate on pubs and golf courses that we call hidden gems?** We have played often at the upscale courses in the states, like the Hilton Heads, Pinehursts, Marcos Islands, and Kapaluas, but often we find the more interesting courses are the unsung, unknown local courses. For example, a favorite of ours is the public course in Moab, Utah, the Moab Golf Club. It's a wonderful, desert-style course where the deep green of the fairways contrasts with surrounding red-rock canyon walls. This course won't make very many "best course" lists in the mainstream golf media, yet it is full of interesting holes, and beautiful views, and it's inexpensive and uncrowded. In short, it adds up to a great golf experience. We found this to be true in Scotland as well. As majestic as the Gleneagles Kings Course is, the Crieff Ferntower Course, only twelve miles away, can provide as satisfying a golf experience at less than a fourth the price. The difference between the famous and the unknown courses is often the amount of their advertising budget and the non-golf amenities they provide.

Acquainttances from our home club return from golf tours in Scotland and Ireland talking about the famous courses they played, or about the tour group members they played with. We come home talking about the fascinating golf we found and about the posties (postal workers) we played with at St. Fillans, or about the late-night round I played at Crieff's Dornoch Course when I was the only player on the course. Others come back talking about the extravagant fees they paid at to Royal Troon, Turnberry, or Loch Lomand. We come home extolling the enjoyable, inexpensive golf that can be found all over Scotland.

As for pubs, Edinburgh and Glasgow have some lively, historic pubs which shouldn't be missed by any traveler. For instance, The Golf Tavern in Edinburgh looks out onto the links, and has good English-style pub grub served in comfortable surroundings. Anne and I enjoyed a delicious courgette (baby zucchini) and Stilton soup at the Bad Ass Bistro, right next to Dirty Dick's, just off the Royal Mile. But we enjoyed it with hundreds of other tourists. Most of those tourists missed the opportunity to eat lunch at the more hidden Myrtle Inn in Collander with a lovely little lady who each day takes her one meal out at the Inn.

Out of the way golf and pubs put us in touch with the real Scotland populated with real Scots. And as Robert Frost said in "The Road Not Taken," "...that has made all the difference."

A third question it would be fair to ask is, **What do we mean by hidden or out-of-the-way?** For golf courses there are easy answers. "Out-of-the-way" means a course that is not on the British Open Rota, one that doesn't require a tee time reserved a year in advance, or one that is not in a metropolitan area. So, courses which are out-of-the-way include some famous courses like Royal Dornoch, Macrihanish, or Crail Golfing Society as well as courses only locals know about like Comrie or Dalmally. Out-of- the-way pubs are even easier to define. If it's not in Edinburgh, Glasgow, Dundee, Aberdeen, or Inverness, then it's fair game for this book.

Next, we should note **what we looked for in both pubs and golf courses.** With over 550 golf courses in Scotland (probably 400 or more fitting the description of "out-of-the-way"), and many times that number of pubs in Scotland, how did we select or deselect those for this book?

In pubs, we include only those we've visited in our six months of Scotland travels, and we include only those that have something positive to recommend them. Though we haven't found too many pubs we haven't enjoyed, we did visit some, like one in Golspie where we stopped for lunch, about which we said, "Naw, let's not tell anyone about this one." In general, we looked at several considerations when evaluating a pub for inclusion in this book:

- Menu – breadth and uniqueness
- Libations – particularly numbers of beers, ales and malt whiskies
- Atmosphere or style
- Service – friendliness and efficiency
- Wholesomeness – a general feeling of "would I bring my mother here"

For golf courses, again we stick to courses we've played over the last five years. And though most courses have something to recommend them, we've played one or two we couldn't find enough good about. Again we designed a list of criteria:

- Quality of shots – both interest and playability
- Condition of the course
- Availability to visitors
- Beauty of the course or surroundings
- Cost or value

These criteria for pubs and golf courses had to add up to a place that both Anne and I, each of us with our different perceptions, could recommend.

Now that you have an idea of the **WHY** and the **WHAT** of this book, a final question might relate to **HOW we gathered the information here presented.** More than six months of travel by car gave us great opportunity to sample both Scottish pubs and golf courses throughout much of the country. Certainly, we haven't explored every corner of the country (although we hope to eventually), but we have covered quite a bit of ground, often more than once. We tried to visit different pubs and play different courses when we covered ground a second time, but often found that we just had to return to a favorite. I don't think we could possibly go to the Black Isle without a stop at the Fortrose and Rosemarkie course. And anytime we're in the West Linton area, we try to stop at the Golden Arms, if not for dinner, then at least for a brew or dram.

The question-asking and note-scribbling often meant we got funny looks from pub patrons, wait staff, or course attendants. And though we got some quizzical expressions, we never had an instance when we didn't enjoy full cooperation from the business people. In several cases when I'd ask for information about a golf course, the pro or secretary would give me a copy of the written history of the course (often published as centenary histories).

Now, with some of the questions out of the way, join us as we prepare for a brief tour of some hidden gems of Scottish golf courses and pubs.

Chapter Two:
Things You Need to Know about Scottish Golf, Pubs, Driving, and Touring

On our very first day in Scotland we ended up spending a couple of hours in the downtown Glasgow shopping district. After a long plane ride and hassles with finding our first lodging, the first thing we wanted was a drink and a snack other than airplane peanuts or pretzels. We stopped at the first pub we could find, took a seat in a booth, and sighed, "Our first Scottish pub!" Then we waited, and we waited. And with, I'm sorry to say, typical American impatience, we began to think we'd never get served. About that time we awoke from our travel-addled stupor enough to see that others were served when they went to the bar. So, off I trundled and ordered drinks and a snack. Almost before I returned to the booth, a waitress had brought us our drinks. That was the first of our "I-wish-I'd-known-that-before" examples.

This chapter is dedicated to even more of our "I-wish-I'd- known-that-before"—all discovered during our six visits to Scotland.

GOLF

Golf isn't the same in Scotland as it is in other countries. That statement is probably true about any golf area. But you've come to Scotland to play golf, and it will help to understand some of the ways golf in Scotland may differ from golf at your home. Here are some aspects of, for want of a better term, Scottish golf culture.

The Courses

1. To play golf you must find the courses. We've discovered several resources you should get to help you navigate the country looking for golf courses. Obviously, you need a good map or atlas. We found Frommer's *Road Atlas Britain* (we took out England, Wales, and Ireland) clearly describes routes and pinpoints golf courses. *Scotland A-Z: Visitos' Atlas and Guide* has also been a helpful road reference. A more specialized map is "Golf Courses in Scotland" (Scottish Tourist Board, 1995), which not only has routing, but also information about each course. The problem is that the map is no longer in publication. Old copies might still be found in travel agencies, or the pro at a local country club might have a spare. That's how I got mine. Also, a magazine called the "Official Guide to Golf in Scotland" (published yearly by VisitScotland) can be picked up for free at almost any Tourist Information Centre. The Guide has details about each course and some notes about directions.

2. Course design and toilets are important, perhaps more important than directions to the courses, especially if you're over fifty. Many of the eighteen-hole courses, except the most modern, are out-and-back designs. The first nine holes play away from the clubhouse, and the second nine play back in to the clubhouse. This means a couple of things. First, you cannot a play just nine of the eighteen, as you can on most courses in the states. Playing only nine would put you at the furthest point away from the clubhouse. Second, it means that either you best be well relieved before you begin your round, or be prepared to answer nature's call in nature. Many Scottish golf courses, both nine and eighteen, lack toilets on the course. At Pitlochry Golf Club we found a ladies' port-a-potty on the tenth hole, but none for men. And at West Linton on the thirteenth a convenient stand of trees (with a path leading to the center) awaits the needy golfer. I personally don't find anything wrong with the system (or lack of it), and Anne has adapted well, but it's an important detail to know if you're going to play golf in Scotland.

3. Perhaps the shortage of toilets forewarns the scarcity of drinking water as well. Many of us are used to water fountains or jugs of water spaced throughout our rounds. In Scotland, water fountains are few and far between. Crieff Ferntower has drinking water between the ninth and tenth holes, but then it has toilets there as well. On Pitlochry GC we found a pipe with water flowing out into a ditch. A metal cup was chained to a post next to a sign, which read, "Drinking Water." I bet the water was straight out of a spring, but Anne wouldn't let me try it. I didn't argue. (Choose your battles.) Plan to carry water on most courses.

4. You will also find it difficult to find power carts (called "buggies"). On several of the more well known courses, buggies are only available with medical certification. Those courses which do have buggies may have a limited number available (St. Fillans Golf Club had only two buggies). In fact, a number of the smaller courses (the subject of this book) didn't even have pull carts (called "trolleys") for hire. Be prepared to carry your clubs if you want to play those courses. Thankfully, for those not used to carrying, the weather is cooler in Scotland, and it's usually the short nine-hole courses which don't have trolleys.

5. Another amenity hard to find on Scottish golf courses, especially the older courses, are yardage markers. Some courses will mark at 150 yards to the green, but many have no markers at all. Americans are spoiled. Golf is really a different game without markers at 200-150-100 yards or when every sprinkler head doesn't indicate a yardage. I find that when I don't know the exact yardage I tend to underestimate and, thus, often end up short. Many 18-hole courses do now provide yardage books, but at $3 to $5 each it really adds to the expense of the golf. Also, it's important to check the card to see whether the hole is marked in yards or in meters. In Ireland, most courses play in meters, and a few do in Scotland as well. It's important to know whether that 150 marker (presuming there is one) is in yards or meters — the difference is 15 yards or almost two clubs! If you find that you are playing in meters, use this easy formula for conversion: Add the first two numbers of meters to the distance and it will equal yards. For example: 150 meters plus 15 equals 165 yards. Another way is to simply add ten percent to the meters to get yards (10% of 150 meters is 15; add together to get 165 yards).

6. Many of the courses you will play in Scotland will be flat and easy to walk, especially links courses (built on the land that links the sea to the land). But be prepared for Scottish descriptors such as "undulating." Peebles Golf Club is considered an "undulating" course, but it is a pretty stiff climb up to the top. Then it drops down and climbs back up. Read "undulating" as "hilly," and consider a buggy when the course is described as "hilly."

7. A fascinating feature of the old Scottish courses, especially the small-town nine-hole tracks, is that holes often cross over other holes. At Corrie GC, on Isle Arran, the first fairway crosses the ninth near the green, and the second near the tee box. We found several such courses where we had to be aware of golfers on other crossing holes. Check the map of the course so that you are forewarned. I didn't pay attention well enough at Whiting Bay, and after teeing off at one hole, I walked right into the landing area for the tee shots from another hole. The golfers yelled a warning at me and apologized, I was the one who needed to apologize. Check the course carefully.

8. Finally, the courses in Scotland are categorized by the types of terrain over which they play. In the States, most of our courses would are designated as parkland or forest courses. In the Southwest we play on desert courses. What will you play on in Scotland? We've noted, and use as descriptors, several different types of courses (briefly described):

Parkland: *a mixture of pasture, meadows, and forest*
Linksland: *played on and in the dunes next to the sea*
Moorland: *combination of tough grasses, heather, and gorse*
Heathland: *similar to moorland, but drier with more heather and often birch forest*
Clifftop or seaside: *played beside the sea, but usually on high plateaus with more park or moor vegetation*
Inland: *a combination park, moor, and heath*

Playing the Course

1. Don't expect to always find a pro shop on the smaller courses. Most will have some sort of clubhouse and changing rooms, but the amenities of a pro shop (golf balls, tees, pencils, snacks, etc.) may not be available. Often no attendant is available to collect fees. Instead, you may find some sort of "honesty box," a place in which you put fees before you go out onto the course. Scorecards are usually near the honesty box, as well as sign-in sheets and tickets. It's a lovely concept for these out-of-the-way courses. At Tarbat Golf Club near Tain in northern Scotland we couldn't find the honesty box in the office, but we did find a sign-in sheet, and with it was the money from players ahead of us. We signed in and left our money, took a ticket and a score card, and went to play. After our round, we visited with two locals on the first tee who asked if we'd found the honesty box all right. I said I hadn't. We both went in to the open office, and he showed me the box in a corner. I showed him the sign-in sheet, the money from the group ahead, our money, and money from a group behind still sitting on the office desk. Honesty Box: out-of-the-way Scotland, yes; in the US, I don't think it would work.

2. On the subject of paying and playing, it may be important to note that many courses, especially the nine-holers, offer only an all day ticket price. For Anne and I, it made nine holes at Innerleithen Golf Club a little pricey (20GBP, or Great Britain Pounds, about $35 US, each). While we had only time for nine, that price was good for play all day.

Eighteen or thirty-six holes for $35 is a decent price. The all day ticket price is a very good deal if you can play more than one round, but not a great deal for one round. But then, it is Scotland, you are on vacation, and who else do you know who can say they've played Anstruther Golf Club on the Fife?

3. If you want to play some of the famous, or famous out-of- the-way courses, be prepared to show a handicap certificate. At Macrihanish, Royal Dornoch, and North Berwick we were asked to prove that we had handicaps of no more than 24 for men and 32 for ladies. Boat of Garten GC requires a certificate also, but we've never been asked for it. We take both our current USGA GHIN cards, which shows our Handicap Index, and our membership card for our home course (though we've only used it once, and that was in England—see Silloth on Solway GC). Be prepared.

4. Also be prepared with lots of ammunition. Gorse eats golf balls (and hands and feet, if you try to retrieve your ball), heather eats balls, and so does most of the rough in Scotland. And there's acres of gorse (also called whins), heather, and grassy rough on the courses you'll play. The ocean seems to pluck balls out of the air. It doesn't seem to, it does! Be prepared to lose golf balls in more than your usual quantity. At one hole on Anstruther GC on the Fife, I launched two balls straight into the Firth, and bounced another off the fairway into the Firth. And I still think of it as a fantastic hole. Plan that you may lose two or three (for a low- to mid-handicapper) balls per round. On the days you don't lose that many, it means more for the next course. But don't get cocky! I played the first sixteen holes at the tough Dornoch Championship course with the same ball. On the seventeenth I thought I might make the whole round on the same ball. Of course, that was the wrong thing to think. I could swear that ball eating gorse bush just jumped into the middle of the fairway to grab my ball. Golf balls are expensive in Scotland, so plan to bring plenty.

5. Speed of play is a concern for golfers everywhere. In the US, five- and six-hour rounds are not unheard of, and four-hour rounds seem to be the target. In Scotland we found that four hours is way too slow. We've seen Scots walk off the course because their round was approaching three-and-a-half hours. Anne and I, and our B & B host, Jacky, worked hard to stay ahead of two 75 year old Scottish newlyweds who were carrying their clubs. Scots also believe in the "honors" system. Quick play and honors may not seem compatible, but if you're ready to shoot when it's your turn, the round can move right along. Two other conditions may account for speedy play in Scotland. First, Scots play a lot of two-balls (pairs or couples) with-out pairing up. A twosome can move more quickly than a foursome.

Not as many players may be on the course, but those who are move faster. Second, when we've played with Scots, the tendency is to give a lot of putts. It made more sense when the handicap system used in Scotland was explained to me. Of most importance, only scores used for calculating handicap are scores in competitions. That means that the casual round of golf in Scotland is not considered an official score, whereas the USGA says players should turn in scores for every round for handicapping purposes. The unintended effect is quicker play. Be careful when you come home, though; after a month of Scottish golf, we find that we are that much less tolerant of slow rounds at home.

6. Before playing in Scotland, you may want to work on the run-up or bump-and-run shot. At my home course (Arrowhead Golf Club, Molalla, Oregon), which I think is a fantastic course, I can't usually play a run-up. Either an obstacle fronts the green (water or sand), or the grass is too heavy or the ground in front is too soft. In Scotland, the majority of holes allow the golfer to run the ball up onto the green from quite a ways out. On the other hand, many Scottish greens are not very receptive to high shots because the greens are too hard or too swaled. The few weeks before we head to Scotland, I will practice the run-up shot on the driving range and the course. Although it may not work well at home, practicing with a six iron from 30 yards out helps my Scotland golf.

7. Though golf won't be cheap in Scotland, costs can be kept reasonable. Some courses offer special prices at twilight, or after a certain time in the afternoon. Playing at those times can save 25 to 50 percent. Another way to save up to half your fees is to take advantage of various reduce-price offers. Certain regions offer special reduced fee passes for courses in the area. For instance, a Borders *Freedom of the Fairways Passport* gives special three- or five-day golf breaks. Other areas have similar deals. On a wider scale, several two-for-one schemes allow you to play on many courses at half price. Green Fee Saver is one we've used for several years to get half-price golf in both Scotland and Ireland. We've also used Open Fairways in Ireland. Two other voucher systems are GreenFree and 2-Fore!-1. All theses programs are available for purchase on-line, or at participating golf clubs. Enough golf clubs, including Boat of Garten and Tain, participate to make it worth your while to at least investigate the programs. For more information:

Green Fee Saver < greenfeesavers.com >
GreenFree, 2-Fore!-1, and Open Fairways < golfalot.com >

8. Finally, our most important suggestion is to play "vacation golf." By this we mean have fun. Enjoy the golf and the surroundings, and don't get bothered by score or performance. One of my worst golfing days was at Boat of Garten GC in the Highlands. I played terribly—so badly, in fact, that I actually quit playing and just walked with Anne for a hole and a half, then dropped a ball and chipped and putted. Whether it was from bad biorhythms or too much driving doesn't matter. I hated my golf, but I loved the course. I count Boat of Garten as one of my favorite Scottish courses, and can't wait until I play it again. Whatever it takes to have fun is what we suggest you do: Take a mulligan (as long as it doesn't slow play), drop one instead of hunting through the heather, dismiss penalties for unknown hazards, etc.

What to Bring for Golf

1. Think about the golf clothes you'll need to bring. Shorts can probably be left at home no matter what time of year. It may be warm enough on occasion for shorts, but they are not a necessity. Rain clothes and umbrellas (*brollies*) are. If playing in the spring or in the fall, long john tops (maybe even bottoms) are not a bad idea; they're lightweight and layer well. I've often been thankful that I had two or three pieces of rain wear (two zip jackets and a pullover), a warm hat with ear flaps, and winter gloves. Plan to play at 60 degrees in the sun, and at 45 degrees with a 30 mph wind and rain, all in one round. It helps if your golf clothes do double-duty as touring clothes, as well.

2. There are ways to pack light on golf clubs, too. On some trips, Anne and I will share one bag and each take six or seven clubs and a putter. Sure, we get into situations where we are under- or over-clubbed, but that's a fun challenge. It's also much easier to take one set of clubs than two. I'm now looking for two small carry bags that will fit into one travel bag. Another suggestion, made by golfer/analyst Johnny Miller, is to take your driver, your putter, and one favorite club, and then rent. Sounds good, but be warned that some of the rental sets at small courses are in poor condition. However you do it, you can pack light and still play golf.

3. Finally, plan to take a camera (even the point-and-shoot throw-aways). The Scottish courses and countryside are beautiful with sites on the courses (castles, ruins, standing stones, monuments, water fountains, etc.) that you won't see other places and will want to show your friends. Film or memory is cheap, so take lots of pictures.

PUBS

A dramatic difference exists between the pubs of Scotland and the services they provide to the community and the taverns or bars in the United States. For the most part, at least with the pubs we'll be telling you about, you can forget the image of a seedy dark bar with down-on-their-luck patrons huddled behind their cheap booze (B-grade movies help create wonderful images). These bars occur in Scotland, like they do in every place, but most of the town public houses (where the term "pubs" came from) are family friendly establishments which serve as eating and meeting places, as well as drinking places. Here is some advice to help you enjoy your Scottish pub experiences:

1. Don't expect typical American bar or restaurant service in a pub. You may get it, but more often than not, you'll be expected to take care of yourself. Many establishments will have menus sitting at the bar or posted on the wall. That's a clue that you may have to ask for service or put your order in at the bar. In most of those cases, the meal or drinks will then be brought to your table. At one pub, though, the drinks were simply brought to the closest part of the bar with the indication that I should pick them up. Whether a wait-staff is helping you or you are ordering at the bar, don't be afraid to ask for what you need (eg., sauce, water, etc.). We now have no problem with this system. We usually sit down to see what a particular pub will do, and then go with the flow. But it is good to know that you can sit in a pub, practically forever, and no one will bother you.

2. When your food does come, it will be HOT! All hot food is served really hot in Scotland, on hot plates. Plan on time for food to cool, especially soup. This is not just microwaved (zapped) hot food slapped on a plate; it's hot food placed on an oven-heated plate. Perhaps it's because Scotland is a relatively cold climate, but whatever the reason, be prepared, food will be HOT!

3. Also be prepared to be given ample silverware. Silverware and serviettes (napkins) come with each course, and are then taken away. To me, it sometimes seems wasteful. I could use that fork and knife for a starter and the main course. But, in almost all cases, the wait-staff will take it away and replace it with fresh. Don't be surprised or bothered by this.

4. While you will get plenty of silverware, you won't get much water or ice. Ask for a Coke and you may get a can and a glass with no ice. Ask for a coke with ice, and you may get a cube or two in the glass. Water is almost as scarce. In most areas of the States, water is served with all restaurant meals. In Scotland, you need to ask for tap water, unless you want to pay for bottled. We get plenty of water when we ask

for a pitcher of water. Our first trip to Scotland was our first trip out of the country, so we wanted to be prepared. I bought a heavy water jug with charcoal filter so we would be safe. Duh! Scotland is famous for its wonderful water—the main ingredient in Scotch whisky. We never used the water jug (It's stuck away in a closet someplace waiting for our trip to Africa). In Scotland, we've never had any ill effects from the food or water. But you have to ask for the water.

5. Expect both dogs and children in the pubs. These are family places and, in most, both dogs and children are welcome. Both, though, may be surprising to see. We've never seen a discourteous dog in a pub; they've all been well-behaved. Some have belonged to the pub and others to patrons. We can't say we haven't seen ill-behaved children in pubs, but it is unusual. Laws govern when children can be in a pub, but these laws are fairly liberal. About the only incident that gnawed at me was, when in a pub in Lamlash (Isle of Arran), I watched a boy of about eight get a pint for his dad. I had to remind myself that this is a different culture.

6. Three notes about food are in order. First, the daily or nightly specials at a pub are often the best bet for quality and price. Most of the time we've been very pleased with what was listed as the "special." Second, the quantity of food in Scotland's pubs is such that you can often get away with just ordering two starters. But if you do, be sure you specify that you want them as starters, and not main entrees. In one hotel pub (not recommended in this book) I ordered soup and another starter. I ended up being charged for the second starter as a main, because I could have shared the potatoes and veggies that came on the side with Anne's main course. Be specific. Third, also be specific if you plan to share something. At the Byre Bistro in Kenmore (a very nice pub) we ordered the pate´ starter. We each got our own starter. To be clear, we needed to say that we wanted to share one pate´ starter.

7. If you enjoy *Uisge Beatha*, the Water of Life (Scotch whisky), we have a suggestion that might add a little surprise to your pub visits. At different places we'll ask the barkeep to select a whisky for us—maybe his favorite, or one representative of the area. It's a good way to start up a conversation, and it has yielded interesting results. About half the time we've done this, we've been given Highland Park from the barkeep. If you want a little adventure, and you can see there's a good selection of whisky at hand, give it a try.

8. Lastly, we offer some advice on tipping. Many guidebooks say it isn't necessary or expected. This is changing. In a pub where you basically get it yourself, no tip is necessary. But after talking with many waitstaff, we found that tips are becoming a more important part of their income. For limited service, a pound on the table may be enough. In a

The road through Sma' Glen is a typical Highland road.

At St. Fillans, if the golf shop is closed, put your fees in an envelope, drop it through the honesty box slot in the door, take a score card, and play away.

This road on the Fife is one of many small tree-lined roads in Scotland.

Pub dogs, like this one at the Golden Arms in West Linton, add an interesting dimension to many of Scotland's out-of-the-way pubs.

pub or restaurant with full service, ten percent of the bill should be left as tip, and more for special service. It may be a sign that some of Scotland's quaintness is vanishing, but this may have certain benefits.

DRIVING

If you are going to find hidden gems of golf and pubs, you will have to drive out of the way. That means the steering wheel will be on the right-hand side of the car, the rearview mirror is to the driver's left, and cars are coming at you from what you perceive to be the wrong side. In six trips to Scotland, I've driven more than 22,000 miles in rental cars. In that time, I've hit bushes on the left a couple of times, hit one fence at a corner (no damage to fence or car), and scared passengers or myself only a few times. I did fold up an outside mirror by scraping a rock bridge in Ireland, but driving in Ireland is an entirely different experience. These experiences have led us to offer you some advice that we wish we had heeded before first driving in Scotland.

1. Obviously, drive on the left. Don't think of it as the "wrong side," but as the "other side." Driving on the left has a major implication: Look Right! One of the hardest concepts to grasp, when walking or driving, is that you must look to the right because that's where the traffic will be. I like the Glasgow Airport's approach which marks all crosswalks: "Look Right" or "Look Left," depending upon which side of the street you are on.

2. When parking, pay attention to the lines on the side of the road. Double lines mean no parking, and single lines mean limited parking. Other than that, anything goes. You'll see cars parked both directions on both sides of the street. In some places you'll see cars parked on the sidewalk. The system makes sense. Why let a parking spot go to waste simply because it's on the other side of the street? Take it, but then remember to drive on the left.

3. Scots will park on both sides and they will stop anyplace they want. I have passed up many a fine photo opportunities because I can't get myself to simply stop the car unless there's a pullout. We approached one car stopped in our lane on a narrow two-lane road as its driver was reading a map. I waited until the road ahead was clear, and then pulled around. It's really not a problem, just not our usual way.

4. Plan on paying more for gas (*petrol* to the Scots). Petrol is far more expensive in the UK than in the States. I'm not very good at converting litres to gallons, but I figure we pay about $5.00 per gallon in

Scotland. Plan that in your budget. Believe me, when we get home, we don't complain about our gas prices for a long while.

5. Plan more time than you think to drive from one place to another. The roads in Scotland, though superior to Ireland's, are still small and narrow, without much room at the edges. You will be driving on the left side on unfamilar roads. Trips will take you longer than you're used to. Twenty miles of back roads in America may take only twenty minutes. In Scotland, twenty miles of back roads may take you thirty or forty minutes. Plan accordingly.

6. Learn to love traffic circles or roundabouts. We are starting to see this type of traffic control system in America, but it is well in use in Scotland. Instead of approaching a corner with cross traffic, you'll come to a circular road, usually around a small island. Traffic enters the circle from the right and exits left onto roads coming off the circle. Three to five roads may spoke off the circle. Your jobs are to enter the circle without disturbing the flow of traffic, and exit onto the proper road. Most of the time, stop signs are not present where you enter, but you are expected to give way to traffic on the right. Remember, you are going left around the circle. After you've driven through a few roundabouts, they make more and more sense. I find they are very efficient. It did take Anne (the navigator) and me (the driver) a while to agree on how to give directions. At first, Anne would say to turn right toward such-and-such. She would be reading a map and seeing the turns as right off the circle, but in reality all the exits are left. Finally, we agreed that she would direct me to "take the second road," or "the second left." Traffic circles are scary at first, but with use will come comfort. Besides, one of the beauties of the traffic circle is, if you don't take your turn the first time, just go around the circle again.

7. Lastly, when you find yourself driving on single track roads, follow the proper etiquette when passing oncoming vehicles. The car nearest the layby, or pullout, gives way. If the pullout is on your side of the road, pull into it and stop until the other car passes. If the pullout is on the other side but you are closest, stay on your side, but stop across from the center of the pullout and let the other car use it to get around you.

I feel quite comfortable now driving in Scotland. It only takes a few minutes on their roads to be comfortable again. I find that the Scottish drivers are courteous, even if they do drive very fast. And one final trick: Have your navigator hold the map up high so all the locals know you're a tourist. They'll forgive a lot.

TOURING

Whether golf is your primary reason to visit Scotland or a sidelight, you will most probably do "that tourist thing." We offer a couple of hints to aid you as you tour the many sights of Scotland.

1. The National Trust of Scotland and Historic Scotland are two umbrella groups working to perserve Scotland's places and buildings of historic significance. Battlefields, castles, nature preserves, buildings of historic importance, and gardens are a few of the sites being maintained. To pay for the work of restoring and maintaining these antiquities, a small admission is often charged. Make use of the National Trust for Scotland (NTS) and Historic Scotland (HS) bargain tickets. When you visit your first site that is maintained by NTS or HS, you may choose to purchase a limited membership (usually three-day, seven-day, or four-teen-day) or a yearly membership. These memberships allow you entrance into all the sites under the auspices of that organization. If you intend to visit several of the sites maintained by that group, the price of the membership will pay for itself. Be aware, though, that some facilities are privately maintained by their own trusts, and your bargain tickets won't help you at these (Glamis Castle, for example).

2. As I mentioned in the Introduction, the Scottish Tourist Information Bureau ("The I"), located in almost every village of size is a great resource for the traveler. Here you can book lodging for a small fee, get loads of free information about the country or the region, buy maps and books, get postcards and stamps, and ask for directions. We found the staff to be very friendly and helpful. Almost all maps will designate which villages or town have an "I." For the golfer, be sure to pick up the yearly *Official Guide to Golf in Scotland*.

3. It's not necessary to take travelers checks or carry large amounts of Sterling. We purchased 500GBP before our first trip, but found that there were ATMs on almost every corner (only a slight exaggeration). It also makes a difference which card you use. VISA is almost universally accepted, Master Card slightly less so, and others are less readily accepted. You can save some money using a bank card. Some cards will charge as much as three percent to convert to foreign currency, while others will charge as little as one percent. Check your cards and shop around for the best price. One nice feature is that the major banks of Scotland don't charge a fee for the use of their ATMs, so the only charge is from your own bank. And if you are going to rely on bank cards for much of your spending, we have an additional hint which comes from experience. In both Ireland and Scotland, we've had our bank put a hold on the use of our credit cards, first at ATMs and then at the tills. This was not because we exceeded any limits, but simply because some of our purchases were

unusual. For instance, in Scotland I made a hefty purchase of whisky and in Ireland we used our credit card to make several phone calls (booking several days of lodging). Both of these triggered some hidden sensor in the credit card computer that said, "We'd better check with these people." It's not a bad policy that the company checks unusual purchases, but they informed us by sending a letter to our home, saying we needed to call them or they would cancel our cards. We're in Dublin and the letter is sent to our home in Oregon. The first we know of the problem, is that our card will no longer work. To clear it up, all we had to do was call the bank verifying that we, indeed, had made the purchases. But that involved making an international call, including waiting on hold for as long as a half hour). To avoid this happening to you, consider telling your card company ahead of time that you will be gone on a trip, and not to cut off your funds because of unusual purchases. On vacation, you really don't need the frustration of funds suddenly drying up—unless you overspend, and then you deserve it.

With these hints about golf, pubs, driving, and touring in mind, let's now do some touring.

Chapter Three:
Central Scotland around Crieff

Golf: Crieff Dornoch, Crieff Ferntower, Comrie, St. Fillans, Killin, Kenmore, Taymouth Castle, Strathtay, Muthill, Auchterarder, Muckart, King James VI, Murrayshall, Murrayshall Lynedoch, Sterling

Pubs: Arduthie House Hotel, Meadow Inn, Haggis and Sporran, Killin Hotel and Riverview Bistro, Tormaukin Hotel, Byre Bistro, Royal Hotel

Attractions (for when you can't golf): Stuart and Caithness Glass, Huntingtower Castle, Balhousie Castle Scone Palace, Sterling Castle, Drummond Gardens, Famous Grouse Experience and Dewar's World of Whisky, Innerpeffray Library

GOLF

The Old Course at St. Andrews is recognized as the Home of Golf. The King's and Queen's Courses at Gleneagles may be golf's royalty. Prestwick, Royal Troon, and Turnberry represent golf's heritage. But the gems of Scotland's golf, the diamonds, sapphires, and rubies, have names like Fortrose and Rosemarkie, Boat of Garten, Shiskine, Killin, Crail, and Crieff.

While the world may recognize and honor the grand courses of Scottish golf, golfers would be remiss if they didn't seek out the gems hidden in almost every small community in Scotland. Here, on these little known and mostly unacknowledged courses, visitors will find scenic beauty, interesting holes, challenging tests, friendly and accommodating staff, eminently fair prices, and, unlike the big name clubs, Scots on the course.

Perfect examples of the Scotland's out-of-the-way golf gems are available nearby the central Scotland community of Crieff. About an hour from the capital city of Edinburgh and only a little more than that from Glasgow, Crieff (from the Gaelic *craobh* meaning "trees") is a central location for tourism and golf. Perth, only 17 miles east with Caithness Glass, Balhousie Castle (the museum for the Black Watch Regiment), and Scone Palace, provides much for the non-golfer to see and do. And if Perth isn't enough, Sterling, with its wonderful castle and monuments to William Wallace and Robert the Bruce, is only about 30 minutes away to the southwest. In and around Crieff itself, the tourist can visit the Drummond Castle Gardens, Stuart Glass, and Scotland's oldest lending library at Innerpeffray. As central as Crieff is to cultural and historic Scotland, it's just as central to great golfing experiences.

We start our tour of Scotland's hidden gems of golf in central Scotland with two very nice courses which lie at the outskirts of Crieff—**Crieff Golf Club's Dornoch and Ferntower** courses. On the A85 heading towards Perth, the Crieff Golf Club is located on the east edge of town. Both courses occupy land overlooking the Strathearn (valley of the River Earn), but they differ in size and history. If you only have time for a short stop, visit the Dornoch nine-hole course designed by St. Andrews golf professional Old Tom Morris in 1891. The course carved out of what was once East Ledbowie Park is an easy walk that climbs gently to the sixth green, then comes back to the pro shop and impressive clubhouse. The featured hole may be hole six, the *Colonel*, a 256-yard par 4 which starts with an uphill blind tee shot with a fore bunker at the top of the hill. The second shot will be into a relatively flat green guarded by a bunker left. From this green are nice views south towards Gleneagles Resort and west towards the Ferntower layout.

If you have the time, the Ferntower course is the one to play. This eighteen hole track, opened in 1980, has the beauty to satisfy any golf tourist, and enough challenge for even the most skilled. Playing the Ferntower course one day with local Bed and Breakfast owners John and Jacky Clifford, I asked about the accessibility of these small courses to visitors. The Cliffords told me that Crieff Golf Club, like almost all the local courses, welcomed visitors anytime a competition was not being held. It helped to be playing with local members who could point out nuances of the course. The challenges start at the first, an uphill par 3 of 163 yards (*Beech Knowe*, literally "hill of beeches"), with bunkers front left and to the right of the smallish green. It's an exciting start, but fair as well. On the second hole, with a right sloping fairway, you must try to keep your tee shot on the left side. Not only is the second shot easier from the left, the right side of the fairway is home to a fine group of Druid Stones, remnants of one of Scotland's ancient cultures. From the second, the layout winds slowly upwards to the top of the course. There are much appreciated bathrooms ("toilets" to the Scots) accessible from the ninth tee and just past the eleventh green. This is an amenity not found on many of Scotland's out and back eighteen-hole courses. On most courses be advised to be well relieved before you begin your round. The top of the course is also the location of one of Ferntower's best holes, the fourteenth. *Ferny Den* is a lovely 324-yard par 4 which starts from an elevated tee. The first shot travels down to a wide fairway, and the second shot comes back up to a raised, narrow green fronted by bunkers and backed by a steep hillside. As much as the shots will challenge the golfer, the hole offers other attractions as well. Great views of the valley and hills south grabbed Anne's attention, as did the 14th Century ruined stable of Ferntower House just to the right of the tee box. The Ferntower and Dornoch courses are only the start of the fine golf available in the Crieff area.

Seven miles west of Crieff on A85 is the small community of Comrie. This village has a nicely decorated main street, with a profusion of flowers at almost every house and business. On the east side of Comrie on Muirend road is **Comrie Golf Club**. A real "Highlands" feel accents this nine-hole course, which remains today much as it was laid out by Colonel Williamson in 1891. The course, like so many in Scotland, is set on the hillsides. Comrie climbs gently uphill for the first five holes, plays the sixth across the top, and from the seventh comes back down to the small clubhouse. While all the holes are interesting, two holes stand out. First is number three, a 174-yard par 3 called the *Quarry*. It's no surprise that the tee shot is over an old fern- and grass-filled quarry to an elevated green. Next is *Monument*, the 493-yard par-5 sixth hole. From the top of the course, with good views of the Lord Melville Monument (a tribute to Henry Dundas, first Viscount Melville who, in effect, ruled Scotland for a time in the late 18th Century), the tee shot drives to a wide fairway. This sets up the second shot, a lay up in front of a green set into a grove of tall trees. The course is worth a second round, but there are more jewels awaiting.

Continue along A85 for six more miles to the next find, the **St. Fillans Golf Club**. This 1903 Willie Auchterlonie tract is mostly flat with nice mountain views. Located at the east end of Loch Earn, the course provides views that may have been the cause of many wayward drives, or, at least, that's what the golfers will say. Anne originally thought the course was fairly easy, but the more she plays it, the more that impression changes. St. Fillans offers plenty of challenge. The only hill on the course comes into play as an elevated tee for the 296-yard par 4 third.

The tee shot must carry 70 to 90 yards of ferns and heather down to a fairway with a bunker on the right. As Anne teed up her ball in about the same place as I had, she noted that the Scots could get carried away with this gender equality idea. The short second shot into a medium-size green must avoid the bunkers right and left. Be sure to take a camera up to the tee box, as the vista is worth burning a little film or memory. It was at this spot, while playing a round with some locals, that we scared up a nice big grouse just down from the tee box. The hill also affects play on number five, called *Bothy* because of the old shepherd's hut on the left. Two Edinburgh postal workers on holiday helped guide us our first time around. Their advice about where to aim the tee shot to cut off a good bit of the dogleg left was almost as good as their advice not to hit long to the forward-sloping green. Anything over the elevated green is bound to be lost. As you make your way around St. Fillans, take in the views of the hills of Glen Lednock to the north and the hills of Glen Artney to the south, but be sure not to miss the the small ruined kirk or church and cemetery off to the left of the long par-four seventh. St. Fillans also has a pleasant tearoom (with great sweet treats) for an after-round or between-rounds bite. While having a bite between rounds on one of our visits, we chatted with Gordon Hibbert, the course manager, telling him we'd lost a small bag of balls out on the course that day. He said, "I put up a sign a couple of years ago which read, 'Lost white golf ball. If found, turn in to pro shop.' It was good for about a dozen balls a week."

From St. Fillans it's about 14 miles (A85 to A827) to one of the most interesting alpinesque communities in the area, Killin. The Falls of Dochart, seen best from the southwest end of town, announces the village. An informative audiovisual history of Saint Fillan is featured in the Scottish Tourist Board's Information Centre. One mile north of the village is the **Killin Golf Club**. This nine-hole course, designed in 1911 by John Duncan for a dedicated group of farmers, tradesmen, and professional people, is a fairly hilly parkland course with brilliant views of the River Lochay and the west side of the Ben Lawers Range. Killin is one of the few small courses in the area which has gas buggies (power carts) to rent. That was important the first time we played because Anne had twisted her foot while on another course, and, though walking was difficult, she wanted to play more golf. Almost all the holes are interesting and scenic, but two deserve special attention. First is *The Dyke*, the 97-yard par 3 fifth. This short, unique hole has a tee shot which must clear a three-foot-high stone wall about five yards in front of a green with a bunker left and a grass mound behind. Visually intimidating, if nothing else. You can be most troubled if your tee shot nestles up to the rock wall, as Anne's did. Bouncing off the wall as I did in the first round, I was at least left with a doable chip shot over the wall. Next, the par 5, 516-yard *Home* hole has been acknowledged by several sources as one of the most picturesque finishing holes in Scotland. It's down hill all the way from the tee box to the 1922 clubhouse and small restaurant. The first and second shots for most golfers will be blind (but the fairways are generous). The third shot throws in the pleasantly distracting views of the surrounding hills and the Lochay Bridge, with a swiftly flowing river beneath. When you play Killin, be sure to note the old crank fire bell in the middle of the fourth hole. Crank the bell after hitting your second shot to let those on the tee know you've cleared. This is a course which should be played more than once; a little knowledge will definitely be rewarded with better scores.

Continuing the circular route which will bring us back to Crieff, we drive about 18 miles northwest on A827 to the resort community of Kenmore. This scenic drive travels along the beautiful Loch Tay its entire distance. Turn off about four miles from the Killin Golf Club for a worthwhile side trip to the Ben Lawers Mountain Visitor's Centre, where you can learn about the geology of the area and the efforts of the National Trust of Scotland to preserve the fragile mountain environment. In Kenmore two other courses are worth trying out—the **Kenmore Golf Club,** a new nine-hole tract with the quaint Byre Bistro beside the pro shop, and the spectacular **Taymouth Castle Golf Club**. The nine-hole Kenmore course sits in a meadow or glen, surrounded by Highland forests. It was here that Anne remembers first planning her shots so she could clear the stone fences, which cross several fairways. Unless you are pressed for time, Taymouth is the course to play (but that doesn't mean Kenmore isn't worth a visit). Taymouth Castle was one of the first places visited by Queen Victoria and Albert, as British Royalty rediscovered the glories of Scotland in 1842. Even though the castle is in the process of being restored, the golf course associated with it is in excellent condition. The Earl of Breadlebane built the "great house" (Taymouth Castle), completed in 1842, in one of the prettiest locations in Scotland. In 1921, when Taymouth Castle was sold and turned into a hotel, famed golf architect James Braid was commissioned to create a golf course on the grounds. Though changes have been made to the original design, such as the addition of a pond at the fourth, it's still very much a Braid course. The design is fairly flat, with vistas of the slopes of Drummond Hill, Taymouth braes, peaks of Lawers Range, and the most-impressive castle seen from almost every hole. Number one, a short par 4 with a small burn (a small creek or stream) in front of a green guarded by three bunkers and large trees, is a fun start to a round at Taymouth. The fifth, *Lawers*, a 543-yard par 5, is the first real challenge. The tee shot must carry a burn about 200 yards from the tee and avoid bunkers right and left. The second shot is a blind uphill shot with bunkers right and trees left and right. Although the fairway is plenty generous, all but the longest hitters should plan to lay back of the top of the fairway hill. The approach shot will drop down 22 feet to a green, well protected in front by two bunkers on each side and trees back. A tough, but fun hole even the first time around. Number twelve, *Bailie's*, a 444-yard par 4, is another example of the interesting holes to be found at Taymouth. The hole starts with a blind uphill tee shot to a landing area protected by bunkers right and left. The long second shot drops 36 feet to a green protected short right and left by bunkers. There are great views of the castle on the left all along the hole. Another enjoyable hole is the seventeenth, a 330-yard par 4 called *Beeches*. After finishing the easy par 3 sixteenth, known as *Dairy* (A converted dairy building which is now a rental cottage overlooks the sixteenth green.), *Beeches* offers quite a challenge. A row of trees runs the length of the left side of the hole, with a tall beech tree guarding the right side of the left dogleg. A tee shot which stays out of the trees must also avoid two fairway bunkers on the right. The shot to the green, although short, must be precise because the green is guarded by three bunkers and another beech tree. For all its beauty, Taymouth Castle Golf Course offers plenty of exciting golf as well.

After a round at either Kenmore or Taymouth, the trip back to Crieff is a delightful journey, which continues on A827 to Aberfeldy. Here it's worth a stop to view the General Wade Bridge over the River Tay and the Black Watch Monument. Six miles east of Aberfeldy on the A827 is the small hamlet of Strathtay, known for its kayak slalom course on the River Tay. It's also home to the **Strathtay Golf Club,** which is a moorland/parkland, honesty box nine-hole course over a hundred years old. The layout climbs up and around several knocks (hills), and ladies and short hitters may struggle by hitting into hill faces and having the ball stop or roll back. Don't be put off, though. Strathtay has some very interesting holes. The second hole, a 210-yard par 3, has visitors questioning how one should play the it. With forest and burn to the left, and the green tucked back into the left, it's either a lay up to the right or a precise draw into the green. The par 3 third hole named *Corpse* (I know there has to be a story behind that name) is another testing short hole. To play the 169-yard hole, either hit around, or be brave and hit over the grove of beech trees between the tee and the green. I miss-hit my tee shot and, after rattling around in the trees for a while, got my ball spit out to the side, where I pitched on and one-putted for my par. I'm sure that is not the approach I'd take next time. The most unique hole is *Spion Kop* ("The Blind Summit"), the 218- yard par 4 fifth. Yes, a 218-

yard par 4! The hole plays dramatically uphill, with the last few yards a twenty-foot drop to the green. The puzzle is, What club do you hit 210 yards and sixty feet up? Strathtay Golf Club is a course you will want to play more than once to figure out how to score. Returning to Aberfeldy, drive A826 until it connects with A822, then into Crieff via A85. It's a total of 25 miles of the most scenic Highland road.

About three miles south of Crieff on A822, heading toward Sterling, is another of Scotland's village courses. **Muthill Golf Club** in the village of Muthill (pronounced *Moothil*) is a nine-hole parkland course with some hills and a few bunkers in play. Like other village courses, such as Comrie and St. Fillans, Muthill golf Club is friendly and accommodating to visitors. The golf here is basic and enjoyable. The fourth hole, a 276-yard, par 4, doglegs left about 79 yards from the green. The right side is protected by trees, and several bunkers front the green. The first time around, it's hard to know what club to hit off the tee. The longest hole is the 393-yard, par 4 sixth, which begins with a blind drive downhill toward the slightly elevated green with bunkers on both sides. There is a nice view of the village below from the tee. The ninth, a 197-yard, downhill par 3, is an interesting finish to the round. The tee shot plays over the eighth green to a small green protected by two deep pot bunkers. Muthill Golf Club is a good stop for a quick round, with enough challenge for most golfers.

From the turnoff onto A823 about a mile from Muthill it's only eight miles to the Gleneagles Resort, with its three eighteen-hole courses and wee (par three) course. This is not an out-of-the-way set of courses. One very windy and rainy day, we stopped to watch golfers, who had probably made and paid for their tee times months in advance, struggle to play in 40-mile-per-hour winds and horizontal rain. It was a day we chose not to play, and after looking at the sour, wet faces of the Gleneagles golfers, we were glad for our decision. Stop by to see the resort on your way down to **Auchterarder Golf Club,** a mile further south. You can play the parkland/heathland Auchterarder course for about twenty pounds, and be playing literally ten yards from people playing the hundred-pound Gleneagles Monarch's course. There is a little elevation change at Auchterarder, and plenty of bunkers, but nothing is too extreme here. Nothing except the first shot on the first hole! *Deil's Dyke* (aptly named) is a 376-yard par 4 that begins with a tee shot which must thread its way between two stands of trees and clear a stone fence (the Devil's Dyke) about eighty yards out. And all the players coming after you stand at the fence and watch your shot. If this shot doesn't give you first hole-jitters, you're a better man than me, Gunga Din. At the fourteenth, *Punch Bowl,* another dramatic first shot awaits. On this 205-yard par 3 a large, deep, intimidating bunker fronts the green, which is bowl-shaped and very receptive. Make a good shot and be rewarded. Simple golf at Auchterarder GC, and at a fifth the cost of the course next door.

A few miles south from Auchterarder is the **Muckart Golf Course**, a varied group of three nines set southwest of the communities of Yetts o' Muckart and Pool of Muckart. A *yett* is a gate or opening and *pool* refers to the flow of the River Muckart. From A91 just follow the signs. The facility at Muckart Golf Club welcomes visitors anytime, but gives priority to Men's Club on Monday and Ladies' Club on Tuesday. The first time we were there, we chose to play the Arndean course. It's the hilliest of the three courses, and with the Cowden course is the normal eighteen-hole configuration. The Naemoor course, another flat nine, makes up the last of the set. Keith Salmoni, the club pro, said that the three courses could be played in any combination. The Arndean course climbs up to the top at the fifth hole, a 361-yard par 4 named appropriately *Top of the World*. And, although the climb up is not steep, the tee box on this hole does provide some great vistas of the hills surrounding Glen Devon. We teed off to a broad, left-sloping fairway with a line of trees to the right. The second shot is to a slightly elevated (from the fairway) green protected by a fore bunker. The three nines at Muckart Golf Club taken together should be described parkland, heath, and moor because all will be found here. After your round at Muckart, enjoy the views of Glen Devon along A823 and plan to stop at the Tormaukin Hotel and Restaurant for lunch, dinner, or a night's stay.

East of Crieff via A85 is Perth with its several fine golfing opportunities. In Perth itself is a course which should be played at least once, if for no other reason than to say you did it. While the name **King James VI Golf Club** is impressive, the location and pedigree of the course is equally impressive. To get to the course, golfers must walk via a foot bridge over the River Tay to Moncrieffe Island (total of about one-third mile from the town parking area). Only one other golf course in the world is entirely on an island in a river, and that happens, coincidentally, to be in Perth, Australia. The course additionally has Old Tom Morris as its original designer (in 1897). Many of Morris' design elements have been retained in today's course, particularly the fairway and fronting bunkering. King James VI is a flat course that makes for an easy walk. The course is basic, straightahead golf. *Corner*, the 358-yard par 4 fourteenth, is probably the nicest hole on the course. The drive on this dogleg right needs to avoid the trees right to set up a second shot to the two-tiered green. The golfing at King James VI is pleasurable, even if not too testing, and the people here are friendly. This course is worth a visit. After all, it's location, location, location.

A more testing challenge will be found near the village of Scone just north of Perth. **Murrayshall Golf Club** (Off A93, before the village turn right, following the signs) is a modern course designed by Hamilton Stutt, grandson of James Braid's chief foreman. The heritage shows in this 6441-yard par 73 with spectacular views over the Kinfauns Forest and farmland below. The course makes use of the natural slopes of the land, but is never a hard walk. Besides the changes in elevation, plenty of bunkers (some deep) and trees create a shot-making challenge. One player commented that "If the course has a soundtrack it would be the clunk of balls hitting trees and golfers swearing." I didn't find the course that difficult, but plenty of holes kept my interest. The par-5 third is a dogleg left, and the drive needs to stay right to have a shot at the green. Whether it's the second or third, the shot to the green must thread its way through three large fronting bunkers. Another interesting hole on the front is number seven, *Dog's Grave*, a 379-yard two-shotter. A large tree in the center of the fairway (about 215 yards out) makes the hole exciting. Left of the tree lengthens the second shot which must cross a burn to the sloping green. But you can't go too far right or you risk the OB, which runs the length of the hole. Be sure to pay your respects to the two dog graves behind the green. The most open hole on this tree-lined course is the par 4, 416 yard fourteenth. There may not be the tree trouble on this hole, but watch out for thirteen bunkers (at least ten of which are in play for the average player). Avoid the bunkers and you still face a demanding, two-tiered green.

Along with the Murrayshall track the facility has a second course, slightly newer and slightly easier, but still worth a round or two. The **Murrayshall Lynedoch** course shares the clubhouse and pro shop with its sister course. Lynedoch is an eighteen-hole, undulating moorland course set in mature woods. Several water hazards and more than a few bunkers add to the challenge, yet Lynedoch has eight holes with no bunkers. The views are as engaging as those at the Murrayshall course next door. The first three holes are a great, tough start to a round. *Two Mile*, the 369-yard par 4 first, is a severe dogleg right where the second shot is over a double gully with two burn crossings. And if that weren't enough of a challenge, the green is elevated and protected by bunkers right and back. *Heathery Knowe* is the 152-yard third hole, which has an elevated green surrounded by three bunkers. The twelfth hole on Lynedoch is an interesting par 5. It's only 456 yards, but the fairway is winding and narrow. It can be an easy birdie hole, or a triple bogie if you get into the gorse left or go over the drop off right. The two Murrayshall courses are a great pair, both for the quality of golf and the grand views of Perthshire.

Looking back from the green toward the tee at Crieff Ferntower's 14th hole, a wonderful par four called Ferny Den, the ancient stable is just visible on the left through the trees.

The fifteenth at Crieff's Ferntower course starts with a steep drop and a dogleg right.

Huntingtower Castle, west of Perth on the Crieff road, is a typical 15th Century Scottish tower house and is open for touring.

Drummond Castle Garden, near Crieff, is considered one of the finest formal gardens in Britain.

Holly Den, the 198-yard eighth hole at Murrayshall near Scone, is typical of the fine parkland holes here.

The tour at Dewer's World of Whisky in Aberfeldy, provides visitors a chance to view the pot stills used in making Scotland's famous single malt whiskies.

The view of Sterling Castle from the Sterling Golf Course is a stunning distraction for visiting golfers.

Ted Powell, curator and librarian at the Innerpeffray Library, pours over the Drummond family history to help me do research for an article on the family chapel.

Our last club in this area is perhaps the course with the grandest view of all. **Sterling Golf Club** in Sterling, south of Crieff via the A9, was built in 1869 and had Young Tom Morris as its first professional. The course, redesigned in 1966 by Henry Cotton, occupies ground that was known as the King's Park, and was the hunting ground for King James IV. Sterling is an eighteen-hole parkland track which plays on a tilted volcanic plug. The grand view at Sterling GC is that of historic Sterling Castle, towering above the course and visible from every hole.

Thick, sticky rough and fifty-one bunkers create a lot of the challenge of Sterling, but there are fine holes here as well. The par-four, 434-yard ninth, called *The Butts,* starts with a blind tee shot which should stay right of the aiming post. Take an extra club on your second shot to a green with bunkers left and right. *Cotton's Fancy*, the 384-yard par 4 fifteenth, is the most difficult hole on the course. It's a dogleg left, with a green which hooks around the fairway. On your second shot, the fairway swings out to the right, but you can aim straight at the pin. Beware though, the elevation gain adds distance to the hole, and the rough short is very tough. Sterling GC is a fine test of golf in an outstanding setting.

The village of Crieff is central to wonderful golfing adventures whether you head toward the highlands at Killin or the lowlands of Auchterarder. Crieff is also a good base for exploring the other treasures found in the central Scotland area.

PUBS

The Crieff area of central Scotland, besides being an area of interesting golf, is filled with pubs and eateries suitable for an after-round repast, whether midday or evening. In Crieff itself Anne and I discovered several establishments we can recommend. One of our favorites—we go back to it every time we're in the area—is the **Arduthie House Hotel Lounge** on the Perth Road (A85 between Crieff and Perth). Just a wee distance closer to town than the Crieff Golf Club, this guesthouse pub makes a great after-round gathering place, or a fine spot for a nice pub dinner. The decor is pub modern with beautiful dark wood accents and rich red upholstery and carpet. The atmosphere is friendly, and every time we've stopped by a conversation with other patrons was easy to start. The menu was very extensive for a pub, with a full and varied selection of starters for a snack or light dinner. Besides quality and value, one thing that keeps us going back to Arduthie House is owner/manager Nigel McInroy. He gives all the guests a friendly greeting and is an engaging conversationalist. He is also very knowledgeable about whisky.

The first time we went to Arduthie House I asked the barkeep (in this case Nigel) to give us his choice for a good dram. It's a technique I use in many places because the answer you get and the manner in which it is given, tells a lot about the pub. It is a fun way to start a dialogue about one of my favorite topics, Scotch whisky. Nigel selected a Highland Park for Anne and I, after asking us a few questions about our likes and dislikes. In subsequent visits, Nigel and I have had good discussions about the whisky trade including his recommendations for several books on the subject. After one such discussion, Nigel said he had something special for me to try. He gave me a good pour of Balvenie 15-year-old. It was a wonderful whisky, and priced very reasonably as well. When in the area, Arduthie House Hotel Pub is a great place to visit.

A different pub experience can be found at a local family pub, the **Meadow Inn**. Whereas Arduthie House Hotel is a guesthouse, serving both overnight guests and drop-ins, the Meadow Inn, on the A822 toward Sterling, is really a pub/restaurant in the roadhouse style. This family pub, with its low ceiling and stone-fronted bar, serves as a meeting and eating place for locals. Serving typical pub fare, but with nine specials, the Meadow Inn was crowded on the Saturday night we visited. The patrons were a combination of young people starting their Saturday night pub crawl, families out for dinner, and older locals taking up their set stations. One older gentleman sat in a corner booth with his corgi beside him. It looked as though this is where you could find them every Saturday night. The menu had a good number of reasonably priced meals. I had a rib-eye steak with three different vegetables, two styles of potatoes, and onion rings. While the food was not gourmet, it was a hearty meal for the price. The atmosphere is loud and lively, with a pool table and two televisions tuned to sports channels. It was considerate that the eating area, with the quieter booths and tables, was situated away from the "sports bar" area. And even though smokers were numerous, the food area was not smoky, suggesting a good ventilation system. The Meadow Inn may be quieter on weeknights, but we felt comfortable and enjoyed the lively Saturday crowds.

The Crieff Hotel, with its **Haggis and Sporran Pub,** represents a combination of the other two eateries already mentioned. On High Street (Perth Road) at the east end of the downtown section, the Crieff Hotel celebrated its one-hundredth year in 2001. The hotel has both a restaurant side and a pub section, and the same menu is available in both. The modern, tavern-style restaurant has both tables and booths and is fairly bright. The good pub menu had many starter and main entree specials. When we ordered dinner the first time, we were very pleased with the large portions served. The menu also had a great selection of desserts, including Spotted Dick pudding, two sticky puddings, and about nine others. Although weak on single malt whiskies, the Haggis and Sporran had a good selection of beers and ales on tap, and an excellent selection of reasonably priced wines. The sports bar section was so lively one Sunday we decided to have a drink on the restaurant side. It was just after a big Celtic-Ranger football match, and obviously the winners were celebrating. It was indeed refreshing when the manager came over to apologize for the noise, and to say he was paying close attention to, as he put it, one "particularly loud bloke." The Crieff Hotel, as well as the Meadow Inn and Arduthie House Hotel, are just a few of the eateries to be found in Crieff. But while out golfing or sight-seeing in the area, many more choices are available for lunches and dinners.

Not for away from Crieff is bit of old England in the form of **The Royal Hotel** in Comrie. This hotel established in 1787, takes the "Royal" in its name from a visit by Queen Victoria as she was exploring the Highlands. The decor is one of rustic elegance, with leather or richly upholstered chairs, and fine art or historic photos adorning the walls. In a separate building is a pub called the Royal Bar. This pub has its own menu of the normal pub fare. The main hotel has its own bar and restaurant, which are both more upscale than the Royal Bar. In both, though, one of the main attractions is the extensive selection of single malts available. At one time there were as many as 170 malts, though the number is less now. The restaurant menu included both ala carte and full dinner items, and was fairly standard, with some variations like steak and kidney pie, and veal topped with fried egg and artichoke hearts. Label this one as elegant pub dining, unless you choose the Royal Bar, which is a lively, local pub.

Killin, a Highland community with an alpine feel and a great little golf course, also has a very pleasant lunch spot. Only about an hour from either Edinburgh or Glasgow, Killin is a natural tourist destination. **The Killin Hotel and Riverview Bistro** on Main Street is a picturesque place to stop, and has been for many years. The Hotel and Bistro situated on the Lochay River has served as a refreshment stop or halfway house for the coach run between Aberfeldy and Tyndrum since the 17th Century. The Royal Stewart Lounge Bar is set in hunting lodge style with round tables, semi-stuffed chairs, and, of course, Royal Stewart tartan carpets. The walls are decorated with old area pictures from as early as 1860. The pub is small and comfortable, boasting an extensive menu during meal hours and sandwiches and soups in between. The Scotch Broth and roll I had really hit the spot after playing eighteen holes at the Killin Golf Club. The wait-staff was friendly, and we chatted quite a while about our trip and the events of the day. This was only a few days after the September 11, 2001, attacks on New York, Washington, and

Pennsylvania. I will give a suggestion: Ring the service bell hard if you're visiting off hours, as staff seems quite a ways away. As we left the Killin Hotel, we stopped for a moment to enjoy the view of Lochay River before it enters Loch Tay.

Heading the other direction from Crieff to play at the Muckart Golf Club, we heeded the advice of some other B&B guests we'd talked to. They said there was a wonderful place to stop along Glen Devon called the **Tormaukin Hotel and Restaurant**. We're glad we took their advice. Tormaukin was a great find, well worth the trip down the Glen. The Tormaukin Hotel and Restaurant, whose name means "Hill of the Mountain Hare," is three miles north of Yetts of Muckart on A823, or five miles south of Gleneagles Resort. Owner Alex Simpson has established a rustic feel at Tormaukin, with beam ceilings, stone walls, and a working stone fireplace in the small pub room. The larger restaurant section is decorated with old photos of the hotel and the area. This "old photo" theme is one we've seen repeated in several places. It's a design feature I enjoy because it enhances our appreciation of the history of the area. When we visited Tormaukin Hotel at midday, a full menu awaited us. The lunch menu offered a delicious mussel, onion, and potato chowder, as well as other specialties. The bar had a broad selection of malts, as well as an extensive wine list in full bottles and splits. While we were eating lunch, a truck pulled up and unloaded a flock of sheep into the fields behind the hotel. We were glad they hadn't suddenly added fresh lamb to the specials. But the sheep unloading did prompt us to ask about the history of the hotel. Originally, it was an 18th Century drovers inn, which had been transformed from a *howff*, where you'd expect to find shepherds stopping to rest their dogs and quaff a pint, into a rustic but upscale hotel and restaurant.

In yet another direction, when visiting the Kenmore or Aberfeldy area, you should stop at **Byre Bistro**. The Bistro, located in Kenmore just over the bridge (follow the signs to the golf course), is just a few steps away from the clubhouse of the Kenmore Golf Club. We've stopped at this pub twice and not been disappointed either time. Byre Bistro takes its name from what was originally a *byre*, or cowshed; now it's a poolroom and small bar. Today, it's a modern, hunting lodge-style pub/restaurant. The pub room is separated from the restaurant side by the bar, which is open to both rooms. Wrought iron and hard wood tables and booths complement stone walls, decorated with quality wildlife prints. It adds up to a very rustic setting. While the selection of malts, beers, and ales is small, it is adequate. The menu is typical pub fare, but several specials are available, even between normal meal hours. On our last visit I had a broccoli and sweet corn soup. I would never have thought of the combination as working together, but the soup was delicious. Both the pub and golf course were converted from a farm. The Bistro was built about 20 years ago, and the golf course about six. In its former life, the golf shop was actually the pig sty.

Whether you are seeking a full meal, lunch, snack, or just a quick pint, many enticing options await you in the Crieff area of central Scotland.

ATTRACTIONS

The politically incorrect saying "Man cannot live by bread alone" could easily be bastardized to "Golfers cannot live by golf and food alone." As much as it might be fun to try living by golfing, eating, and sleeping, there's so much more to do and see in Scotland that it would be a shame to only discuss Scotland's golf and pubs. Before our first trip to Scotland in September, 2000, I hadn't realized the depth of Scottish history and culture. Since that first trip, we've come to appreciate all that is available to the tourist in Scotland. In this part of the chapter, we suggest sights and activities for those days when (not if) it rains too much for golf. These are also ideas for sight-seeing after a quick nine-hole round. In no way do we imply that these few suggestions will exhaust what you can see and do in a given area; as for the Crieff area, our suggestions barely scratch the surface of the possibilities.

Starting in Crieff itself, **Stuart Glass**, a working crystal factory, on A822 towards Muthill, is an interesting stop. Here you can see glass being blown and visit a nice display shop. For a different kind of glass factory experience, visit **Caithness Glass** in Perth (just off A85 as you come into town from Crieff). This factory is world famous for its beautiful, ornate paperweights. At the factory, a viewing area permits visitors to watch the working factory from above. From this vantage point, you can hear all the roar, and even feel some of the heat, of the furnaces as factory workers create their magic. Just like at Stuart Glass, Caithness Glass has a fully-stocked gift shop plus a small cafe. While in Perth, three historic buildings are among the sights to visit. The first, **Huntingtower Castle** (off A85 about a mile west of town), is a fairly complete double towerhouse, built in the late 1400s. Huntingtower, or as it was known before the 17th Century, the House of Ruthven, has a well preserved Eastern Tower and Western Tower. The roof parapets are accessible and provide fine views of the countryside. Within Perth is **Balhousie Castle**, off Hay Street. This castle now houses the museum of the Black Watch Regiment, one of the oldest regiments in Scotland, having been formed in 1783. The history of the regiment is told in several floors of displays of military memorabilia and art. This is an educational stop, even for those not normally interested in military history. A couple of miles north of Perth on A93 is the third, and most impressive, of the historic buildings, **Scone Palace** (pronounced "skoon"). Restored in the 19th Century, this home of the Earl and Countess of Mansfield was the original residence for the Stone of Destiny (also called the Stone of Scone), which was used as a coronation throne for Scottish Kings since King of the Dalriada Scots, Kenneth MacAlpin, brought it to Scone Abbey in 838 AD. The Stone is now housed at Edinburgh Castle along with the Scottish Crown Jewels. Scone Palace has several rooms open to visitors, a beautiful display of fine porcelain, and a most impressive Royal Gallery which houses a world-famous collection called *The Vernis Martin* (paper mache *objects d'art* made in the 1730s by the four Martin brothers). On the Palace grounds the visitor can find a path named for David Douglas, who was born at Scone. Along the path are many of the plants discovered by Douglas, and the country's first tree that was given the name Douglas fir, grown from a seed sent home by the famous botanist. Plan to spend a morning or afternoon at Scone Palace.

Another royal residence dominates the city of Sterling. Historic **Sterling Castle** sits atop the volcanic plug of Castle Rock in the very heart of Scotland. It has been a royal residence since at least the 12th Century, and possibly earlier. William Wallace defeated the English at the Battle of Sterling Bridge just below the castle in 1297, and Robert the Bruce again defeated the English within sight of the castle in 1314 at the Battle of Bannockburn. However, most of the current buildings date to the 1400 and 1500s. There is much to see at Sterling Castle, and major restoration work is almost complete on the impressive Great Hall. Also plan to visit two gardens, the Queen Anne Gardens within the castle walls, and the King's Knot, outside the west wall between the castle and the Sterling Golf Club. We've visited the castle several times and find something new to us each trip.

Closer to Crieff is another outstanding botanical experience, **Drummond Castle Gardens**. The magnificent gardens are rated by many as among the best in the UK. Laid out by the second Earl of Perth, John Drummond, in 1630, they are well worth a visit. The impressive castle on the grounds, regrettably, is not open to the public, but is still interesting for its mixture of 15th Century and Renaissance architecture.

Once you feed your aesthetic spirit, it might be time to indulge a different kind of spirit, Scotch whisky. Two nearby distilleries will provide assistance. The first, only a couple of minutes drive west of Crieff, is **The Famous Grouse Experience** (formerly Glenturret Distillery), Scotland's oldest, established in 1775. The home of Famous Grouse blended whisky, Glenturret also has some fine single malts which are hard to find in the U.S. The tour, as with most of distilleries open to visitors, is very informative, and especially interesting is the story of Towser, the distillery cat who is listed in the *Guinness Book of World Records* for catching over 20,000 mice in his lifetime. A statue to Towser stands outside the very nice gift shop. The last stop on the distillery tour is at the tasting room where, for all your hard work at listening and learning, you are rewarded with a dram of the local product. The Famous Grouse/Glenturret also has a small bar and restaurant. If you enjoy your dram, you might consider ordering a sampler in the bar, which contains four tastes of different Famous Grouse whiskies. If you do, be sure that you don't have far to drive. Another nearby whisky distillery is the **Dewar's World of Whisky** in Aberfeldy. This distillery, home to the Dewar's line of blended whiskies, is also the producer of Aberfeldy Single Malt Whisky (again, not easily found in the U.S.). This is an interesting self-guided tour with many interactive exhibits. One very convenient feature on the tour was an e-mail station from which I could easily send a postcard. It was positively evil of me to send a postcard from a whisky distillery in Scotland to the work station of a teaching colleague in America. Evil, but fun!

Our last suggestion may seem like we left the least interesting for last. In reality, we saved the best for last. A visit to the **Innerpeffray Library, Chapel, and Schoolhouse** is a must as far as we're concerned. This is Scotland's oldest lending library and is still used for research and genealogical study. Situated on the River Earn, four miles southeast of Crieff on B8062, the library is a trip back into history. It's also a trip down a single track road, at least for the last half mile. On one visit, we were following a slow-moving car, and could not figure out why the car was creeping. Then I spotted a whole bunch of little feet underneath the front of the car. Scurrying along just ahead of the car was a covey of grouse, going as fast as their little legs would take them. They never did fly, but finally scooted off the road, under a fence, and into the field. We have visited Innerpeffray three times, and each time the curator/librarian, Ted Powell, has shown us wonderful old works being preserved in the library. On one visit we saw a 16th Century world atlas which showed the West Coast of the U.S. above San Francisco as a squiggly, featureless line running up into the unknown. On another visit, we saw a 15th Century "bestiary," with descriptions and paintings of all manner of beasts. For example, a rhinoceros depicted as a beast wearing armor plates was obviously drawn from a description of a rhino as an animal with thick, armored hide. The setting for the library, chapel, and schoolhouse is isolated now, but originally it was on a major Roman road. When the bridge over the River Earn collapsed in the mid-1800s, and was later rebuilt several miles away, Innerpeffray became the outpost it is today. The library is not open all the time, but brochures available at the Tourist Information Centre in Crieff and at many B&Bs will tell you the schedule. Indeed, if you find you have the time, Innerpeffray would be first on our list of fascinating places to visit around Crieff.

GOLF COURSE INFORMATION

Course: **Crieff Dornoch**
Style & Length: Parkland, 2386 yds, par 32
Price: 10GBP (Great Britain Pounds)
Availability: Easy to get on
Phone: (01764) 652397
Web: www.crieffgolf.co.uk

Course: **Crieff Ferntower**
Style & Length: Parkland, 6402 yds, par 71
Price: 30GBP
Availability: Easy to get on except on competition days
Phone: (01764) 652397
Web: www.crieffgolf.co.uk

Course: **Comrie Golf Club**
Style & Length: Moorland, 3020 yds, par 35
Price: 16GBP/18 holes
Availability: Easy to get on
Phone: (01764) 670055
Web: www.comriegolf.co.uk

Course: **St. Fillans Golf Club**
Style & Length: Moorland, 2898 yds, par 34
Price: 16GBP/day
Availability: Easy to get on
Phone: (01764) 685312
Web: www.st-fillans-golf.com

Course: **Killin Golf Club**
Style & Length: Parkland hilly, 2351 yds, par 66
Price: 15GBP/18 holes
Availability: Easy to get on
Phone: (01567) 820312
Web: www.killingolfclub.co.uk

Course:	**Kenmore Golf Club**
Style & Length:	Parkland, 3026 yds, par 35
Price:	8GBP/9 holes
Availability:	Easy to get on
Phone:	(01887) 830226
Web:	www.taymouth.co.uk/golf

Course:	**Taymouth Castle Golf Club**
Style & Length:	Parkland, 6066 yds, par 69
Price:	22GBP
Availability:	Fairly open, call ahead
Phone:	(01887) 830228
Web:	www.scotland-golf.co.uk/golf-course

Course:	**Strathtay Golf Club**
Style & Style:	Moorland/Parkland, 2041 yds, par 32
Price:	12GBP/day
Availability:	Easy to play, no trolleys
Phone:	(01887) 840211

Course:	**Muthill Golf Club**
Style & Style:	Parkland, 2340 yds, par 30
Price:	13GBP/18 holes
Availability:	Easy to play
Phone:	(01764) 681523
Web:	www.muthillgolfclub.co.uk

Course:	**Auchterarder Golf Club**
Style & Length:	Parkland, 5778 yds, par 68
Price:	20GBP
Availability:	Fairly open, call
Phone:	(01764) 662804
Web:	www.auchterardergolf.co.uk

Course:	**Muckart Golf Club**
Style & Length:	Heathland, Arndean nine hilly, Arndean 2835 yards, Cowden 3251 yards, Naemoor 3234 yards, par 71
Price:	17GBP
Availability:	Easy to get on
Phone:	(01577) 840595

Course:	**King James VI Golf Club**
Style & Length:	Parkland, 6038 yds, par 70
Price:	20GBP
Availability:	Call ahead
Phone:	(01738) 632460
Web:	www.kingjamesiv.co.uk

Course:	**Murrayshall Golf Club**
Style & Length:	Parkland, 6441 yds, par 73
Price:	27GBP
Availability:	Call ahead
Phone:	(01738) 554804

Course:	**Murrayshall Lynedoch Golf Club**
Style & Length:	Parkland, 5361 yds, par 69
Price:	27GBP
Availability:	Easiest of the two Murrayshall
Phone:	(01738) 554804

Course:	**Sterling Golf Club**
Style & Length:	Parkland, 6438 yds, par 72
Price:	28GBP
Availability:	Busy, call ahead
Phone:	(01786) 464098
Web:	www.sterlinggolfclub.tv

Chapter Four:
The Highland Road –
Up the A9 to Dornoch and North

GOLF: Pitlochry, Blair Atholl, Kingussie, Boat of Garten, Grantown-on-Spey, Fortrose & Rosemarkie, Tarbat, Tain, Royal Dornoch, Golspie, Brora, Helmsdale, Reay

PUBS: Taybank Hotel, McKay's Hotel, Moulin Inn, Loch Tummel Inn, Old Bridge Inn, Speyside Heather Center and Clootie Dumpling, North Kessock Hotel, The Eagle Hotel, Mallin House Hotel, Southerland House, Bunillidh

ATTRACTIONS (for when you can't golf): Shopping (Pitlochry, Aviemore, Made In Scotland), Distilleries (Edradour, Dalwhinnie, Glenmorangie), Castles (Blair, Cawdor, Dunrobin), Historic Sites (Clava Cairns, Culloden)

GOLF

Scotland's Highlands are the prototypical Scottish landscape; a land of sweeping mountains of heather, fern, and rock. A rugged, imposing landscape, full of adventure, intrigue, and romance. A great way to experience the Highlands is to take a trip up the A9 (Scotland's main north-south motorway) from Perth north. All along this route you will find interesting golf courses, pleasing eateries, and wonderful tourist attractions.

We start the A9 golf adventure in Switzerland. At least that's how **Pitlochry Golf Club** is known, and for good reason. At this Highland eighteen-hole course they don't rent buggies (it's too steep for them) and they don't rent normal pull trolleys (too steep); instead, they hire out electric trolleys (called caddy carts) to help you climb the hills. When I rented one for Anne, she was a little put out, saying the cart was more bother than it was worth. She changes her mind as the course kept climbing. She did draw my attention to the two-some behind, who were struggling to pull a wayward caddy cart out of a deep bunker. Don't get the idea that this is an impossible climb; it's not. I carried my clubs even though I was huffy and puffy a few times, but I was 57 and more than a few pounds overweight. Pitlochry G. C., designed in 1909 by Willie Fernie of Troon, is a parkland course which plays up the side of a mountain (or at least it seems that way). The slope does become a condition of play with many uphill, downhill, or sidehill lies from which to hit. The course's other main hazard is its strategic bunkering. Number six, a 378-yard par 4, is called *Druid Stone* for the ancient stones found just off the green. On this hole you tee off from a very elevated tee box, with the ladies tee even higher (Anne loved that), down to a wide fairway with a stand of trees left and a bunker in play left for long hitters. The second shot continues down to a green protected all around by five bunkers. *Druid Stone* is historic, fun and challenging. The fourteenth is another downhill test. This short 284-yard par 4 has plenty of trouble available on the tee shot, including hummocks and hillocks in the fairway, trees left and right, and a small burn further left but still in play. The second shot must negotiate more swales to a green protected back and right by bunkers. Then you turn around and go back uphill on number fifteen, *Drumcroy*, a 300-yard par 4. Your tee shot needs to pass a grove of trees on the right that act as a natural ball magnet. If you've left yourself in good position off the tee, the second shot is to the green protected only by the hill,—Oh yes!—and by the bunkers left and right. The tee shot on eighteen has a nice view, since its straight downhill to the welcoming clubhouse. After our round, we visited in the clubhouse with three golfers who had played in front of us. All were English transplants to Pitlochry who really loved the course and the town. They gave us some good advice about pubs and B&Bs in the area. All in all, Pitlochry Golf Club is a quality course with spectacular views of the Tay and Tummel Rivers and the Tummel Valley.

Heading north from Pitlochry, it's seven miles to a parkland nine-hole course not far from Blair Castle. The **Blair Atholl Golf Club**, founded in 1896, is a course that's easy to walk and worth a visit. Bunkers are scattered around the greens and fairways, and two ponds come into play. Other than those hazards and a few trees which can cause trouble, the course is simple, yet fun. Number three, a 308-yard par 4, shares a green with the 508-yard, par-5 ninth. On both holes your shot into the green must clear a 20-foot rise to find the green. The sixth is a tough 245-yard par 3 with five bunkers protecting a medium-size green, but there is room to run the ball up between the bunkers. I played Blair Atholl with my friend Grady, who chipped in his fourth shot on the ninth from about ten yards off the green for a birdie. Several club members were standing outside the clubhouse bar watching us play. When the chip went in and the crowd applauded, Grady hollered, "My first birdie in Scotland!" One of the members watching said, "Laddie, we have a tradition around here that whenever someone makes their first birdie, they buy drinks for the whole clubhouse." Grady would have, too, if his wife hadn't taken all their travelers checks with her to the Castle. I'll have to remember that tradition on my home club.

Continuing up the A9 for another thirty-five miles, you will arrive at Kingussie (pronounced "king-YEW-see"). To find the eighteen-hole, parkland/heathland **Kingussie Golf Club**, turn at the Duke Hotel and follow the signs to the caravan park. The first nine here was opened in 1891. Harry Vardon then designed the second nine in 1908. The club has a lovely clubhouse (built in 1911) and lounge, which seemed to be the liveliest place in the village. The course has only one par five and six par threes (5615 yards, par 67) and rough that can cost you a stroke or more if you tangle with the gorse or heather. Anne loves that the course plays over a varied topography; several holes play through a meadow, then several are on a hillside, and finally, you play back down toward the meadow. On number six, a 325-yard par 4 called *Shepherd's Hut*, your first shot must be accurate because the hill encroaches on the left and heavy rough waits on the right. If your tee shot is decent, the second shot is short but must negotiate a significant dip in front of the green. The views of the Monadhlieth Mountains from the sixth green and seventh tee are stunning. Speaking of the seventh tee, the first shot from this elevated tee box must carry the Gynack River and avoid the large bunker left. Pick the correct club here. After completing the shortest par three at 105 yards (the fifteenth), you must hit to the longest. The tee shot must carry the fields of gorse and heather and climb up to an elevated green. Heavy rough is all the protection this hole needs. Kingussie Golf Club was a surprise to us. We hadn't heard much about it, but certainly enjoyed playing the course and intend to stop again. In fact, the beauty of the course made its way onto television via the BBC's *Monarch of the Glen*. Anne and I were watching one episode where two of the main characters are shown out on the local golf course. Anne saw twenty or thirty seconds of the course and said, "That's the clubhouse, first, and fourth hole at Kingussie." We couldn't confirm that Kingussie was the course they used on the show, but Anne has an almost photographic memory for every golf course she's played (which is great, because all I have to do is show her a photo of a hole and she can give me all the details).

From a Harry Vardon course, we move further into the Highlands to a James Braid gem of a design. **Boat of Garten Golf and Tennis Club,** called "The Boat" by members, is one of Scotland's golf jewels. The community of Boat of Garten, about three miles off A9 on A95, is named for an early ferry crossing spot on the River Spey. The village is small, but the golf course is a grand test, in a beautiful setting. The views are superb , and the Cairngorm Mountains seem only a fairway wood shot away. James Braid designed the course in 1932, using the natural contours of the heathland to create interesting holes as well as aesthetic views of the Cairngorms. For a premier golf course, The Boat is relatively short at 5866 yards from the medal tees and 5650 from the member tees. Don't let the lack of length fool you, there's plenty of challenge here. Braid's bunkering directs the line of play and heather, broom, and birch trees provide the rest of the trouble. The first hole seems to be a bit of a let down. You're here to play a gem of a course and it starts with a flat, boring, one-shotter. From there on the course gets more interesting and more difficult. The fourth and sixth holes pass near the tracks of the Strathspey Steam Railway, which takes tourists the five miles between Aviemore and Boat of Garten and adds a wee bit of romance to the course. The chug and whistle of the train may be the only thing that will disturb the peace on the course; that and the oaths of golfers who stray off the fairways. The 163-yard par 3 third hole, *Craigard*, is a difficult short hole with rough fronting the green and a steep drop off to rough and trees right. The sixth, *Avenue*, is probably the most challenging hole on the outward nine. At 403 yards, this par 4 demands that you stay in the fairly narrow fairway to have a chance at the green protected by two bunkers. The tougher holes are on the inward nine with the fifteenth, *Gully*, being the most unique. This 307-yard par 4 requires a short lay up to a plateau, which leaves a second shot of about 150 yards over a gully to the green. It is the eighteenth, though, that is recognized as the most difficult hole at The Boat. *Road* is a long par 4 (437 yards), with the second shot to an elevated green which runs off on all sides. A lay-up, leaving a wedge to the green, may be the prudent shot. As challenging as Boat of Garten course is, one golfer who'd been playing on the links courses in the Fife noted that the course made a good contrast to the famous links courses. Anne says that it's a course that makes you want to play it again and again. Indeed, Boat of Garten Golf and Tennis Club should be on the play list of anyone wishing to experience good Scottish golf.

Near to The Boat is another enjoyable heathland course, **Grantown-on-Spey Golf Club**. Built in 1890, this undulating course with eye-popping views, several burn crossings, and plenty of bunkers has been termed "a challenge to all golfers." It's hard to describe a couple of holes that will represent a "feel" for the entire course, because they are all so good. Grantown is, also, an enjoyable ladies' course. Anne points out that straight and down the middle works well here (I'll have to try that sometime.) Number nine, *Murphy's View*, is probably the most picturesque and finest short par four in the area. At only 275 downhill yards, it's easy to go for the green, but be warned: Bunkers and rough both right and left wait for any missed shot. This hole is also special for the spring-fed water fountain at the tee box. It's some of the sweetest water you'll ever taste. Every time we play, we fill extra bottles so we'll have plenty in the car. Another special feature of Grantown is Shaw, the starter/pro shop manager. He's one of the friendliest golf staff we've ever met. We almost missed our tee slot visiting with him.

The north Highland area is really James Braid country. As we moved from The Boat and Grantown, we next found another Braid masterpiece on the Chanonry Point of the Black Isle (not an island, but a peninsula just north of Inverness, noted for its black soil). The **Fortrose and Rosemarkie Golf Club,** named for the two nearby villages, has been called "a gem of a course," and "perhaps the brightest jewel in the Highlands golfing crown." I'm not sure I'd call it the brightest jewel; we haven't been to Royal Dornoch yet in this chapter. I will say, though, it is one of my favorite courses in Scotland. Golf has been played on the land at Chanonry Point as early as 1700, though the current course wasn't designed by Braid until 1888, then extended in 1935. As opposed to The Boat, this is Anne's stereotype of old Scottish links golf, with all the holes playing on a spit of land (the Point) jutting out into the Moray Firth. With eight holes playing beside the Firth, and the rest of the holes playing in the linksland between the shores, all the elements of traditional links golf come into play—wind, weather, gorse or whin. The beach is in play, and not impossible to hit out of as I found out one round on the second hole. There are many interesting holes at Fortrose (pronounced "fort-ress"), but the fourth and fifth stand out. Number four, *Lighthouse*, is a 455-yard par 5 from the medal tees and a 446-yard par 4 from the member tees (unfair!). This tough hole plays along the Firth, but through tall hummocks with a blind second and, for some of us, third shot to an undulating green. The Chanonry Lighthouse is just off the back of the green, but from anywhere near the fairway, don't use it as an aiming point. Especially from the members' tees, bogey is definitely your friend on this hole. *Lighthouse* is followed by *Icehouse*, a tricky 132-yard par 3 which can require anything from a gentle wedge to a wood, depending on the strength and direction of the wind. The hole is named for the old icehouse behind the green, which is out of bounds if you hit too long. It was on the tee box of the sixth that a local we were playing with told us about the dolphins. Steve, an oncologist at the Inverness hospital, pointed out that a pod of dolphins is often seen cavorting in the Firth about this area. Just as he said that, we saw the dolphins break water, not a nine-iron shot off the shore. Hard to hit the next tee shot while watching the dolphins play. I did get to experience playing out of a Braid fairway bunker on my next shot, though. The last hole, *Fiery Hillock*, is a challenging 212-yard par 3 where whin lines the fairway, ready to grab a stray shot. The bunker fronting the green was at one time a mound upon which fires were lit to send disaster news along the Moray coast. In fact, one of the qualities I like best about Fortrose is how steeped in history it is. Besides the *Fiery Hillock*, a memorial stands near the thirteenth hole to mark the spot the Brahan Seer was burned for foretelling of doom and despair which was to befall the House of Seaforth (the local laird). The seer's predictions came true. A marker also exists where you want to land your tee shot on the 355-yard par 4 seventeenth, and marks the spot on which the last witch in Scotland is reputed to have been burned. At the end of the round be sure to visit the nice clubhouse where your green fees make you a member for the day. All clubs allow visitors access to their clubhouses, but it was a special touch to label us "members for the day." Fortrose and Rosemarkie may be a short course, but at about $35 US, it's a fantastic out-of-the-way bargain.

After Fortrose we were looking for something more out of the way. We found it in Portmahomack, about six miles off the A9 on B9165. The nine-hole course at the end of the point called the Tarbat Ness was an enjoyable find. **Tarbat Golf Club** has a small club office, men's and ladies' changing rooms, and an honesty box for you to put your fees in. Established in 1909, this links course makes good use of the land, and the Dornoch Firth is visible from most holes. On hole number five, *Don's View*, a 177-yard par 3, the tee shot must thread its way between two large, deep, steep-faced bunkers to a moderate-sized green. At *Jackie's Brawist*, the 302-yard par 4 eighth, you can see the flag (with the local kirk or church behind it), but between you and the flag are 250 yards of hillocks and hummocks and swales. Play the course a hundred times and you'll have a different lie each time. The lies won't necessarily be bad, just different. Your second shot, from however far out, must negotiate the rest of the swales. Anne thought the course tested her shot-making skills, but she felt successful. The players we met at Tarbat were all very friendly and eager to share their course. Tarbat makes a good, low-key stop in amongst the more high powered courses in the area.

Back on the A9, Tain Golf Club fits the description of "high- powered." On the edge of town and along the Dornoch Firth, **Tain Golf Club** is an 1890 Tom Morris-designed links course with lots of gorse, Scotch broom, 51 bunkers, and several burn crossings. All the holes here are well-designed, but a few stand out. The ninth hole, *Mafeking*, is a 355-yard, dogleg par 4 with bunkers and trees on the inside corner. A lay-up short of the left-hand bunker at 227 sets up a good view of the green. The eleventh, *Alps*, is often called "a great hole." You must drive well on this 380-yard par 4 because your second shot will be a blind shot over a large hill, the Alps. Don't be short of the hill with your second because a large pot bunker will collect shots rolling back off the Alps. A daunting tee shot is the first at *Black Bridge*, the 215-yard par 3 seventeenth. Your tee ball must cross a river twice and avoid the water again as it passes the right side of the green. Tain is championship golf at a reasonable price.

And speaking of high-powered golf, **Royal Dornoch Golf Club** is about as powerful as it gets in the northern Highlands. As one writer puts it, "Although Royal Dornoch is now well established in both serious and romantic golf it still borders on the verge of being a 'hidden gem.'" Located right off the main town square (two miles east of the A9 on A949), Royal Dornoch is probably the best Scottish course not to be on the Open Rota; it's too far out of the way to be the host of a major championship. Its remoteness, though, adds much to its mystique and charm. Here is a topnotch course, on par with the Turnberrys, Royal Troons, and Muirfields, that almost anyone (with a handicap certificate under 25 for men and 32 for women) can play at almost anytime. Although the course is on the list of many tour groups, it's still possible to walk-on many days. The course is on almost everyone's "to do" list and consistently rated in the top twenty in the world, but its remoteness keeps it from being overrun. Its desirability, I'm sure, will increase due to the fine book by Lorne Rubenstein, *A Season in Dornoch: Golf and Life in the Scottish Highlands*, which tells of Rubenstein's three-month stay in the village and his love affair with Royal Dornoch. When Anne and I played in 2002, we played with a Canadian who had come to Dornoch just because of the book, and it was to be his only golf during his trip.

The course itself is recognized as the third oldest links (1616) in Scotland for which written records exist, (St. Andrews, 1552, and Leith, 1593). The club was founded in 1877 when the course was only nine holes. Shortly after it opened, it was redesigned by Old Tom Morris and three years later a second nine was added. Dornoch became Royal Dornoch in 1906 when it was granted a royal charter by King Edward VIII. Royal Dornoch has a strong American connection because the famous American golf architect Donald Ross (Pinehurst #2 and over 600 other courses) was born in Dornoch and played in his formative years at Dornoch. This is a great links course with six holes playing next to the Dornoch Firth, spectacular bunkering, plenty of gorse, quite a bit of elevation change, and few blind shots. The course begins innocently enough with a 331-yard par 4, protected by nine bunkers, heavy rough left and right, and out of bounds further left. As fearsome as this sounds, it really is an easy beginning—the trouble is abundant if you stray, but birdie is available to straight-hitters like Anne (a 24 handicapper). The second hole, *Ord*, a 177-yard par 3, presents more of a challenge. The plateau green is the target, and to miss right or left puts you into deep, punishing bunkers, as Anne discovered. Ah, the fickle fortunes of golf! In fact, Tom Watson was asked to name the toughest shot at Dornoch. He answered, "The second to the second." These opening holes give an indication that fair, tough golf is what is to come in the round. Not a bad hole can be found on the course, and no two are really the same. The sixth hole, *Whinny Brae,* meaning "hillside full of gorse" (figurative definition rather than literal), is a tricky 163-yard one-shotter. Tee shots contend with a plateaued green, a steep hillside of gorse, three bunkers left, a deep bunker front right, and steep drop off back and right. I found the middle left bunker and made what, for me, was a great bunker shot to keep the ball on the green. Bogie can be very good here. Thirteen, *Bents,* is a tremendous par 3 at 166 yards from the white tees. From an elevated tee you hit down to a smallish green surrounded by seven bunkers. Needless to say, get plenty of bunker practice before coming to Dornoch, because you'll get plenty of opportunities while you're here. *Valley,* Royal Dornoch's 405-yard par 4 seventeenth, is a fun hole. The blind drive (aim a little left of the aiming pole) is to a lower tier fairway (40-foot drop) which turns sharply left. The second shot must clear a high bank and avoid three bunkers. The green is relatively benign after the first two shots. If there's any complaint I have about Royal Dornoch, it's about the eighteenth, *Home,* which comes far too soon in the round! Especially if you get to play in pleasant or reasonably nice weather, you don't want the round to end. Anne views Royal Dornoch with mixed feelings: the course is wonderful and frustrating. She'll often hit straight down the middle and end up in trouble—but that's links golf. She still would never miss an opportunity for a round here.

Professional golfers like Tom Watson, Ben Crenshaw, Nick Faldo, and Greg Norman have sung the praises of Royal Dornoch. Other golfers call their experience at Dornoch "remarkable." This is an out-of-the-way golfing experience that is out of this world and worth every effort it takes to make it possible. A second course at Dornoch, the Struie Course, is shorter, easier, and cheaper than the championship course. We didn't get to play it, but after talking with other players, we will try it the next time we're in the area (unless we're playing the championship course).

Royal Dornoch, rated as one of the best in the world, has to be acknowledged as the best course in the northern area, but other good courses exist even further north. First, in the small town of Golspie, 13 miles north of Dornoch, is a surprising course, the **Golspie Golf Club**. I use the term "surprising" not in a disparaging way. We really were surprised at how good the course is. We'd seen it on an earlier trip and always thought it looked rather boring or simple. Don't judge a course only by the holes you can see. When we finally played Golspie in the Fall of 2004, we discovered it is interesting and challenging, especially once we played past the first few holes. Founded in 1889, this eighteen-hole links track plays along the edge of the North Sea, and the sea breeze a major factor. The fifth hole, Sahara, is a short par four along the beach, with a 150 yard carry over rough to a moguled fairway. The second shot is to an elevated green with only the top of the flag visible. The hardest par 3 on the course is the seventeenth, at 217 yards. The tee shot is made more difficult by a large rise in front of the green, protected by a large bunker left. There is a bailout area for those who can't carry the 195 yards to clear the rise. It turned out the first holes were actually more interesting than they looked. We learned our lesson and will not be so quick to judge without a fair trial.

In the village of Brora (meaning the "bridge's river," about a half hour north of Dornoch) is another one of James Braid's fine creations, the **Brora Golf Club**. This eighteen-hole track has hardly changed since Braid planned it in 1923. It is now the headquarters for the James Braid Golfing Society, a group organized to honor Braid, his accomplishments, and ideals. Brora Golf Club is a links course with fine views of the Sutherland foothills and the Kintradwell Bay along the North Sea. It's along this bay that eight of the first nine wind. A quaint aspect to Brora is the electrified fencing around the greens to protect them from livestock, which still graze on this "common land." It also makes for the interesting local rule that says to play cow pies as "casual water." On *Burn*, the 428-yard par 4 fifth hole, the burn flowing down from Clynelish distillery bisects the hole. It may be tempting to taste the burn, but save that for after the round in the pleasant clubhouse. The tee shot should be short of the burn which will leave a fairly substantial second shot to a small green. Number thirteen, *Snake*, is an interesting short par 3 at 125 yards. The name comes from the burn, which "snakes" through the hole. And though the tee shot is short, the green is well-protected by five bunkers. Brora Golf Club doesn't have the elevation changes of Dornoch, nor the Royal pedigree, but it is a fine course worthy of a round or two.

Next, we come to **Helmsdale Golf Club,** a half mile up the A897 from the A9 in Helmsdale. This moorland course, about 12 miles north

The thirteenth at Boat of Garten is a classic James Braid design short par five—a dogleg right with an uphill approach to a well protected green.

One of the most dramatic holes at Grantown-on-Spey is the ninth, a 367-yard par 4 that is all downhill.

Eilein Castle, nesting in Loch an Eilein, is one of the attractions within a few miles of Aviemore in the Scottish Highlands.

The Cairngorm Funicular Railway takes visitors up to the Ptarmigan restaurant at the 3600-foot level.

The Royal Dornoch Clubhouse is good place for a pint after finishing the 18th hole on this championship course.

Pitlochry village is considered the Gateway to the Highlands, and its main street is a series of guesthouses, eateries, tweed and Highland craft shops.

Blair Castle has been the seat of the Atholl Dukedom since the 1200s. Today, the castle has more than thirty rooms open for touring.

The Home hole at Brora Golf Club is a difficult 18-yard one-shotter.

of Brora, is Scottish golf at its most basic, and an interesting change from the Sutherland links courses. The nine-hole Helmsdale course is cut into the side of a hill and makes good use of the terrain to create interesting holes. There's nothing fancy about Helmsdale, though the original 1920's clubhouse does at least have a toilet. Pay your fees by putting them in the mail slot of the house across the street. An abundance of gorse covers the course, and several holes have grass-covered rock walls (dykes) crossing fairways. The second hole requires a very delicate shot. It's only 82, yards but the green is protected by a small bunker in front and by OB five yards past the green. The seventh, called *Plateau* (238-yard par 3), plays uphill, with the green hidden by a rock wall about 100 yards out from the green. As if uphill 238 yards isn't protection enough, the green has a bunker left. We were about the only players on the course on Saturday at midday, except for a young lad who followed us up two and three, and then went into the house between the third green and the fourth tee to have lunch. Later in the round we did stop to chat with an older gentleman who was walking the course with his two dogs. One of the dogs is a ball hunter, and he said that after a tournament day, the dog can find half a dozen balls or more on a walk around. Helmsdale Golf Club isn't a course I would recommend as a golfing destination, but neither would I steer you away from it. If you're in the area and want to experience rural Scottish golf, it makes a interesting (Anne calls it "funky"), quick round.

But to really experience out-of-the-way golf, continue up the A9 to Thurso, and then on the A836 to Raey and the **Reay Golf Club**, the most northerly golf club on mainland Britain. Again a James Braid design will challenge your shot-making skills on this 5831- yard par 69 layout. Not the length, nor bunkers, nor rough are too extreme. They don't need to be. What is extreme is the wind which can be 20-30 miles per hour on a calm day! We played when the wind was howling at forty to fifty per. Number six, *Braid's Choice* (Braid often named his favorite hole on the courses he designed.), is a 477 yard par 5 gentle dogleg left. It's definitely a birdie hole, since it pays downwind most of the time. The back side is more interesting than the front, and one of the more interesting holes is the thirteenth. *Spring Lochy* is a 305- yard, downhill par 4 with almost no fairway. Watch your tee shot carefully so you can find it in the light rough. The green is in a hollow, with two pot bunkers fronting right and left.

The A9 route up through the Highlands to the north area is peppered by magnificent, out-of-the-way golf. The courses along the A9 range from simple, small village golf at Helmsdale, to some of James Braid's finest works at Boat of Garten and Brora, to world-class golf at Royal Dornoch. Just driving up or down the A9 and playing the nearby courses could be a golfing vacation in itself, but there's much more to the region than just golf, as we will see.

PUBS

Along the A9 corridor, most of the golf courses have pleasant club-houses which serve meals most of the day. We found Pitlochry, Kingussie, Fortrose, Dornoch, and Brora all to be good stops for drinks and/or meals. We also found some other very delightful stops along the way.

The community of Dunkeld is not really in the Highlands, but at 13 miles south of Pitlochry, it's close. Besides, it's right on the A9. The Dunkeld and Birnam Golf Club is one we want to try on a future trip, but a pub in Dunkeld is a must-stop for anyone traveling along this section of the A9. **MacLean's Real Music Bar,** in the Taybank Hotel in Dunkeld, is the closest we've found to an Irish pub outside of the larger cities. Just off the main street of town as you cross the River Tay, the Taybank Hotel has a beautiful view of the river. That would be enough to call for a stop here, but there's more. This is a music pub decorated with musical instruments, photos of local scenes, and photos of session players. A drink shelf runs all the way around the pub room (just the right height to place your glass), much the same as we saw in most pubs in Ireland. Besides a standing area, small tables with chairs and a few bar stools furnish the room. Traditional music was playing in the background (from tape or CD), but live music is present at least three nights a week. Sometimes the music will be session-style (players perform for themselves and for drinks), but sometimes it's in a more formal setting. Upstairs, a small concert venue, the "Music Gallery," is an option, too. It charges a nominal fee. The night we visited, the charge was six pounds. You can select meals from a small bar menu, which specializes in "stovies." Stovies are stoved potatoes (from the French *etoufee* which means "to stew in a closed vessel")—Scotland's meal in a bowl. Several incarnations were available: *Beinn a Chally* (lamb, onions, and carrots), Butterstone (chicken, bacon, peppers, carrot, and onion), Tribute (haggis and neeps or Swedish turnips). There were also soups, salads, toasties, and puddings on the menu. The night we visited was a pleasant fall evening and several diners were eating outside, overlooking the river. MacLean's Real Music Bar is owned by Scottish folk singer Dougie McLean, and should be on any visitor's list, especially if you want to hear traditional music.

We visit Pitlochry often because Anne knows of this killer jewelry store. On our trips, we've found two pubs to recommend. The first is the

McKay's Hotel and Johnny Fox Irish Pub and Restaurant, on the main street of town . The hotel was built in 1890 and has a small bar near the hotel entrance, facing the main street of town. This area has full-bar service and deli-style meals. The eating/drinking area is right on the busy street. In the back, though, is Johnny Fox, which was added a year or two back. Johnny Fox Irish Pubs are a small chain, with other pubs in Inverness and near Balloch on the Moray Firth. Johnny's is a modern pub design; part bistro, part sports bar. Here, as in other Johnny Foxes, are booths with glass partitions and tables arranged for viewing the large screen TV. In Pitlochry, they had a full bar with a good selection of malts, including the local product, Edradour. It's a full restaurant menu with several interesting specials. The Johnny Fox Irish Pub at McKay's Hotel is a safe bet for a meal or a drink. But if you want something special, go a little ways out of town.

A half mile out of Pitlochry on the A924 is the small village of Moulin and the **Moulin Inn**. If the truth be known, the only attraction in the village is the Inn. In the clubhouse at Pitlochry GC over a pint, a couple of locals told us to try the Moulin Inn. "It's the most British-style pub in Scotland," they said. We don't know exactly why it qualifies as a British pub, but we do know it's good. The Moulin Inn (from *Maoil-inn* Gaelic for "bare, rounded hill," referring to a local spot, *Baledmund Hill*) is a very old coaching inn established in 1695. The small bar (no stools, just standing area) had three tables with benches and small stools. The pub is decorated with old photos and a framed collection of old moneys. A real peat fire blazes, and a great old painting hangs over the fireplace. You can eat in the bar (but it's very small), or in the restaurant section with old wood booths and tables. Moulin boasts its own brewery and serves four of its brews (a light ale, Braveheart Ale, Ale of Atholl, and Old Remedy Ale), as well as a selection of about 30 single malts. The dinner menu is strong, with several specials including Venison Braveheart (venison in beer sauce), Crackie Grostel (sautéed potato and smoked bacon topped with fried egg), and Scotsman's Bunnet (batter pudding filled with game and veggies). Anne chose the venison steak, and I the Guinea Fowl Leg—both were very tasty. Wherever and what-ever you eat, you must order at the bar by your table number. The Moulin Inn is definitely on our list as do again dining.

West from Pitlochry is another great pub similar to Moulin. On the shores of Loch Tummel, about six miles from the A9 on B8019, you'll find the **Loch Tummel Inn**. The hunting lodge inn has a restaurant (Hayloft) and a lounge bar (Stables), both of which serve wonderful meals. The specials, such as grilled Halibut Steak on Arbroath Smokie with Gruyere Risotto, are particularly enticing. A pulley system sends orders down to the kitchen, and a dumbwaiter brings food up. Service is friendly and the food delightful. Then step outside and gather in the view of beautiful Loch Tummel. For an even better view of the Loch, drive a couple miles east of the Inn to The Queen's View Visitor's Centre.

We've used Aviemore, about 50 miles north of Pitlochry and 30 miles south of Inverness, as a golf touring base for the past several years. More than fifty courses lie within an hour and a half of Aviemore. While staying there, we've found several rather forgettable eating establishments (which we won't tell you about) and a couple of good ones. The **Old Bridge Inn** behind the rail station is a pub/restaurant with several rooms, including a small bar. Most of the patrons are tourists, but it is a place locals go to as well. The menu is small, but several daily specials, whose quantity is limited, may tempt you. We've seen them run out of two different specials while we were sitting. Emphasis is on quality rather than quantity. I've enjoyed a very tasty roast beef with yorkshire pudding a couple of times. A little more unique dining experience can be found just a few miles out of town toward Grantown-on-Spey. **The Speyside Heather Garden and Clootie Dumpling Restaurant** is a casual tearoom with an extensive menu. Serving cafeteria style, Clootie Dumpling Restaurant offers four soups, a variety of prepared sandwiches, several mains, and tons of sweets each day. The restaurant specializes in Clootie Dumplings, a pudding made with spices, carrots, apples, and raisins, in a pot cooked over an open fire. They serve twenty-one different kinds of the dumplings, including a Heather Cream Special and an Apricot Delight. It's not a pub, but it is interesting dining.

Our next recommendations is up the road, west of the A9 and the Black Isle at North Kessock. Here, along the Moray Firth and almost underneath the 1982 Kessock Suspension Bridge, is the **North Kessock Hotel and the Crow's Nest Pub**. This is a relaxed seaside resort pub and restaurant. One wall of the pub had early photos of the old town and buildings, including the hotel, before a fire burned it down in the early 20th Century. The staff was very friendly, including "Kellie," the pub's Scottie terrier. We've eaten here twice and not been disappointed. The food is good, especially the Cullen Skink (a smoked haddock and potato chowder), and comes in large portions. One evening we enjoyed dinner with John, a retired dairy manager from Manchester who was walking from John o' Groat (the tip of Scotland) to Land's End (the bottom of England). We enjoyed interesting conversations and good views of the Firth and the bridge.

The next three dining suggestions we have are in Dornoch and are particularly for golfers. **The Eagle Hotel's Lounge Bar** is a golfer's hotel pub located on Castle Street, about five minutes walk from the golf course. The main tourist activity in the area is golf, and this 1850 building, recently refurbished inside caters to golfers. In the pub, with a horseshoe of booths and tables around the bar, the conversation is mostly about golf. The Lounge Bar has a very eclectic decor, consisting of Highland prints, old tools and weapons, musical instruments, old photos and posters, and, along the tops of booths, an interesting display of old whisky and liquor bottles. We spent parts of five evenings here, and most of the patrons were touring American golfers. A local woman, though, received the most attention. She had brought her dog, a friendly, lab-dalmation mix, to the pub. A few "What's-a-dog-doing-in-a-restaurant" comments came from some of the tourists. On a different night, the group Skelbo, a local traditional music group who had played at Madonna's wedding, performed in the lounge. This is a lively pub. The food is also a draw. The Eagle Hotel's pub menu is large with two pages of main entrees and one page of starters. Although the menu carried no nightly specials, it did contain some unusual items, including Hunter's Chicken and a delicious Chicken and Ham Pie. Even though there were no nightly specials, the menu did carry some unusual items including Hunter's Chicken and Chicken and Ham Pie (which was delicious!). On a different night, Anne and I each had a tasty bowl of creamy mushroom soup, rich with the flavors of wild mushrooms.

Practically across the street from Royal Dornoch is another great golfer's pub in the **Mallin House Hotel**. The bright bar is decorated with photos of golfers and logo golf balls from around the world. I brought one from my home course to put on the wall. The well-stocked bar has a Malt-of-the-Month special, providing an interesting whisky at a great price. The dining room is decorated with golf course prints and antique clubs. A mashie, which had belonged to Bobby Jones and had been donated by a member of Royal Dornoch, hung on one wall. After a round on Royal Dornoch, Anne and I enjoyed a well-prepared steak and scampi combination.

A final suggestion in Dornoch is the **Southerland House** on the main town square. A little less golferish than the other two, nonetheless, this pub and lounge fills up with golfers telling tales of the day's rounds. It's a comfortable place, with a stone wall dividing the pub from the dining room and the same menu serving both. Service is very good and the food is excellent.

If you want to go really out of the way (maybe when playing at Raey or Helmsdale), eat at the **Bunillidh Restaurant** on the main square in Helmsdale. It's beyond me how a place this good got to be located so far off the beaten track in the far north of Scotland. But I'm sure glad we found it. The restaurant is casual by the very nature of its decor—everything is spread everywhere: figurines, masks, toys, and other fascinations. The real calling, though, is the extensive menu.

Many of the recipes, it is said, date back to the Great Clan Gatherings. For their Aussie friends, the restaurant serves Kangaroo Steaks cooked in whisky. The specialty, though, is fresh seafood, served as fish pie, seafood chowder, or just heaping platters of trawled-that-morning langoustines. The special of the day, when we stopped on our way south from playing at Raey GC, was fresh-caught lobster. We each had a complete lobster, of at least a pound and a half, served with all the trimmings, for less than twenty dollars US! Not only is the food at Bunillidh fabulous, it's inexpensive as well.

Travel the A9 from Dunkeld to Helmsdale and you will find great eating adventures, from lobster to Clootie Dumplings, all along the way.

ATTRACTIONS

As opposed to other locations which I describe in other chapters, this area of Scotland lends itself to groupings of attractions. So, we'll try to take you from south to north, giving you some ideas for shopping, whisky tasting, castle viewing, and history hunting.

Our tour starts in **Pitlochry,** a wonderful Highland village full of exciting shopping opportunities. This self-appointed "Gateway to the Highlands" has a main street lined with interesting shops, such as discount woolen shops, a fine whisky shop, and several souvenir shops, among others. In particular, a visit to the Heather Gems Factory is worthwhile. This factory uses heather wood to create beautiful stone-like earrings, pendants, and broaches. The factory allows viewing of some production facilities, and offers detailed information about its absolutely unique product. Of course, there is a gift shop as well. Keep close tabs on your credit cards, as it's easy to get carried away. A new attraction in Pitlochry is the Scottish Plant Collectors Garden, an extended garden and forest area showcasing botanical species from all over the world. The other shopping town along the A9 is **Aviemore** (about 5 miles south of Boat of Garten). This is an alpinesque village known as a hiking,fishing, bicycling, and skiing center. The shops here cater to the outdoor tourist. This is also the terminus of the Strathspey Steam Railway, which makes a five-mile run between Aviemore and Boat of Garten several times daily. Several holes on the Boat of Garten Golf Club are visible from the train. Further up the A9 at the west end of the Beauly Firth is the town of Beauly (accessible from Inverness via A862 or further on the A9 via A832), named by Mary Queen of Scots on a royal visit. Beauly is a quiet village with a striking Priory, but we direct you here for one shop in particular. Opened in 1991, the **Made in Scotland Shop** is a shopping tourist's paradise. This shop has all manner of

Scottish goods, from food to furniture, from jewelry to books, and from pottery to blankets. It's easy to spend time (and money) in the shop, and the staff is very helpful about making it easy to send purchases home. The Made in Scotland Shop is a worthwhile side trip if you're looking for quality gifts and souvenirs.

A different kind of shopping is available at Scotland's distilleries. If you've gone through the Malt Whisky Trail, you've seen several distilleries already, but on the Highland Road are three good stops to view the distiller's art. The first is **Edradour Distillery** (Edra-dower) out of Pitlochry and past Moulin. Edradour is Scotland's smallest distillery, producing in a year what the larger distilleries produce in a week. Only three workers (exclusive of tour staff) maintain the production process from start to finish, and all live in houses on the distillery grounds. This is how all distilleries at one time operated. The tour is unique because of the size of the facility. As always, a dram of Edradour's 10-year-old malt whisky rewards you for your effort. From the smallest distillery we move up the A9 to the highest. **Dalwhinnie Distillery** in Glen Truim (about 30 miles north of Pitlochry) at over 1000 feet in elevation is actually an official meteorological station as well. The name *Dalwhinnie* is Gaelic for "meeting place," which is fitting for the distillery sits at the junction of old north and west droving routes, used to drive stock to market. We stopped early one morning on our way to a booking on The Boat and asked if we could still have a taste, even if we skipped the tour. The friendly staff said, "No problem," made a good pour and added, "This will help wake you up." The Highland Road is also the route to the home of the best-selling Scotch whisky. **Glenmorangie** (rhymes with "orangy") **Distillery** in Tain, nine miles south of Dornoch, was first licensed in 1843, making it one of the oldest in Scotland. The grounds of the distillery are beautiful and the tour excellent. Glenmorangie specializes in wood-finish whiskies (Madeira wood, Port wood, Sherry wood, among others), and has a bountiful shop to wander while sipping your dram. Even for visitors who are not whisky drinkers, the distilleries here and other places provide interesting notes on the history of Scotland, so intertwined with the *"Water of Life."*

Three castles along the A9 route deserve to be on the tourist's agenda. The first is one of the most impressive castles we've visited, with thirty-two rooms open for viewing (many have only five or six). **Blair Castle** in Blair Atholl (about seven miles north of Pitlochry) is the home of the Duke of Atholl, and has been home to Stewarts and Murrays since it was begun in 1269. The Duke maintains the only private army in the British Isles. Called the Atholl Highlanders, this 80-man force consists of mainly estate workers and serves mostly ceremonial duties. The Atholl Highlanders are actually the sole survivors of the ancient clan system, wherein each clan chief had an army to call upon. Leave at least a couple of hours to tour the open rooms and know that, even then, you won't see everything. One of the highlights of the tour would be the spectacular China Room, with floor-to-ceiling displays of English, Continental, and Oriental chinas. A second highlight would be the 19th Century Ballroom filled with armor, antlers, and portraits. If you have time, the grounds are equally impressive. Be sure to stop to listen to the lone piper, who plays a long set by the castle entrance every couple of hours.

More historic than Blair is **Cawdor Castle,** just a couple miles off the A9 south of Inverness. This 14th Century castle owes much of its fame to William Shakespeare, who in the play *Macbeth* titled the lead character Thane of Cawdor. In the play, Macbeth does in King Duncan at Cawdor Castle to become king himself. While some real Scottish history is presented in the play, Cawdor Castle does not play a part in it. The real MacBeth did bring Duncan's rule to an end in 1040 when he died at Elgin Castle; MacBeth was then crowned King of Scotland at Scone. Cawdor Castle wasn't even built until the 14th Century. Visitors so often ask about the link between Macbeth and Cawdor that the 5th Earl of Cawdor once remarked, "I wish the Bard had never written his damned play!" The castle does display some beautiful 17th Century tapestries and has some nice gardens. A short golf course on the grounds has holes as short as 130 yards marked as par 4s. It might be an interesting break from touring.

Scotland's most northerly Great House can be found near Golspie halfway between Dornoch and Brora. **Dunrobin Castle** is the ancestral home of the Earls and Dukes of Sutherland. Today, many rooms in this 15th Century castle (with additions in the 19th and early 20th Centuries) are open to visitors. Much of the interior was remodeled by Charles Berry, architect of the House of Parliament in Edinburgh, after a fire in 1850. Besides the castle tour a separate museum, formal garden, and a falconry exhibition may be of interest. The view from the second story dining room, overlooking the gardens and the North Sea beyond, is splendid.

"Stunning" might describe **Clava Cairns** (formally *Bulnaraum of Clava*) about two miles east of the A9 and about four miles south of Inverness. The field of three cairns with standing stones was first excavated in 1828 and represents late-Neolithic or early-Bronze Age burial chambers. This dates Clava to before the first of the Great Pyramids (as old as 4400 BC). Cup and ring markings on some of the stones make up the outer face of the cairns. Archeologists can only guess at the meanings of these markings. Set within a beautiful grove of beech trees, Clava Cairns is a truly mystical site.

Only a mile away from Clava is another site of tremendous historical importance. On Drumossie Moor the morning of April 16, 1746, the last battle on British soil took place between Prince Charles Edward Stewart's (Bonnie Prince Charlie) Highland army and the British forces led by the Duke of Cumberland, son of King George II. The **Battle of Culloden** was the last gasp for the Jacobites, trying to regain the crown for the Stewarts. In the short battle, 1500 Highlanders were slaughtered, many by Cumberland's orders as they lay wounded on the bleak moor. The battle and its aftermath was the death knell of the clan system in Scotland; afterwards, the wearing of tartans and playing of bagpipes were banned. Today, Culloden's story is told at the visitor's centre, where an instructional audiovisual presentation explains what led to the battle and the battle itself. Visitors are free to walk to the Drumossie Moor, which has been restored to the condition it would have been in on the day of the battle. Most somber of the memorials here are the Clan Grave Stones, one for each clan which lost members that fateful day. It is also interesting to see the *Leanach Cottage*, a restored 18th Century crofting (farming) cottage next to the visitor's centre.

It seems fitting to end this chapter at Culloden. Here, as in all of Scotland, there is beauty amongst sadness. Here, too, is a piece of a complex, intriguing history of a people who in winter would lay down their farm tool and weapons, and pick up their golf clubs.

GOLF COURSE INFORMATION

Course:	**Pitlochry Golf Club**
Style & Length:	Heathland hilly, 5811 yds, par 69
Price:	20GBP
Availability:	Restricted Sat. and Sun. before 9:30
Phone:	(01796) 472792

Course:	**Blair Atholl Golf Club**
Style & Length:	Parkland, 2908 yds, par 35
Price:	14GBP/day
Availability:	Easy to get on
Phone:	(01796) 481407

Course:	**Kingussie Golf Club**
Style & Length:	Heathland, 5615 yds, par 67
Price:	22GBP
Availability:	Fairly easy to get on
Phone:	(01540) 661600
Web:	www.kingussie-golf-club.co.uk

Course:	**Boat of Garten Golf and Tennis Club**
Style & length:	Heathland, 5866 yds, par 69
Price:	29GBP
Availability:	Contact in advance, requires handicap certificate
Phone:	(01479) 831282
Web:	www.boatgolf.com

Course:	**Grantown-on-Spey Golf Club**
Style & Length:	Heathland, 5710 yds, par 70
Price:	20GBP
Availability:	Busy, call ahead
Phone:	(01479) 872079

Course:	**Fortrose and Rosemarkie Golf Club**
Style & Length:	Links, 5883 yds, par 71
Price:	25GBP
Availability:	Visitors welcome most times
Phone:	(01381) 620529
Web:	www.fortrosegolfclub.co.uk

Course:	**Tarbat Golf Club**
Style & Length:	Links, 2990 yds, par 31
Price:	10GBP/day
Availability:	Walk on, honesty box course, no trolleys
Phone:	(01862) 871598

Course:	**Tain Golf Club**
Style & Length:	Links, 6404 yds, par 70
Price:	33GBP
Availability:	Fairly open, call ahead
Phone:	(01862) 893313
Web:	www.tain-golfclub.co.uk

Course:	**Royal Dornoch Golf Club**
Style & Length:	Links, 6514 yds, par 70
Price:	69GBP
Availability:	Book in advance, handicap certificate required
Phone:	(01862) 810219
Web:	www.royaldornoch.com

Course:	**Golspie Golf Club**
Style & Length:	Links, 5836 yds, par 68
Price:	25GBP
Availability:	Busy, call ahead
Phone:	(01408) 633266
Web:	www.golspie-golf-club.co.uk

Course:	**Brora Golf Club**
Style & Length:	Links, 6110 yds, par 69
Price:	25GBP
Availability:	Visitors welcome but can be busy
Phone:	(01408) 621417
Web:	www.broragolf.co.uk

Course:	**Helmsdale Golf Club**
Style:	Inland, 1760 yds, par 31
Price:	5GBP, honesty box course
Availability:	Welcome anytime, no trolleys
Phone:	(01431) 821063

Course:	**Reay Golf Club**
Style & Length:	Links, 5831 yds, par 69
Price:	20GBP/day
Availability:	Easy to get on
Phone:	(01847) 811288
Web:	www.reaygolfclub.co.uk

Chapter Five:
The Northeast Coast

GOLF: Stonehaven, Torphins, Dufftown, Royal Tarlair, Cullen, Strathlene Buckie, Spey Bay, Elgin, Hopeman, Nairn Dunbar

PUBS: Creel Inn, Gordon Arms Hotel, Three Kings Inn, The Seafield Arms Hotel, Kimberley Inn

ATTRACTIONS (for when you can't golf): Dunnottar Castle, Stone Circle, Whisky Trail, Castle Trail, Baxter's

GOLF

Up the eastern coast of Scotland from just below Aberdeen to about Inverness are some of Scotland's best seaside golf courses. Carnoustie, Royal Aberdeen, Cruden Bay and Nairn are but a few of the famous courses along this stretch of coastline. Also along this route are fabulous courses less well known, but deserving of a visit.

Starting with a visit to the resort village of Stonehaven we find our first interesting course—**Stonehaven Golf Course**. It's just north of the village of Stonehaven, about 15 miles south of Aberdeen along A90. Immediately, you know there's something different about this course. The well-appointed clubhouse with lounge is situated above the course and has wonderful views over the first couple and last couple of holes. The course is not a links course, but it is a seaside course which sits on a bluff overlooking the North Sea. In my mind, I labeled the course a seaside, clifftop course. Some holes, particularly nine through twelve, are very much parkland holes. The rest of the holes play along sea cliffs and face the full brunt of the ocean's influence. The Stonehaven Golf Club, like many in Scotland, dates back to before the turn of the last century. It was 1888 when ten holes were built on a different site, but a year later that was reduced to nine. In 1897 the present eighteen-hole course was laid out, with some additional James Braid improvements in 1906. Your round will start off with the 305-yard, par 4 first hole called *Ruthery*. This is a relatively easy starting hole, yet it gives a real indication of what awaits at Stonehaven. The tee shot should easily clear the mounds in the center of the fairway (about 180 yards), but must avoid the out of bounds on the right, which really cuts toward the fairway at about 210 yards. Two hundred thirty-one yards off the tee on the left is Hitler's Bunker, waiting to catch a long tee shot that strays left. The Hitler Bunker is the remains of a crater caused by a German bomb dropped in August of 1940. The green is protected by bunkers left and right. As you walk down the fairway, you can't miss the ruins of St. Mary's Church to the right. There really are no uninteresting holes at Stonehaven, though the parkland holes (nine to twelve) aren't as distinguished as the seaside holes. Instead of describing one or two holes, I'll discuss the broader features of Stonehaven to give a sense of the course. Several holes have carries over chasms or ocean inlets. Number two, a 203-yard par 3, tees up alongside the cliff edge, with the out of bounds (the cliff) running about half the length of the hole. The course is 4804 yards, par 66, and six, seven, and eight are all par threes, with cliffs along the right side. Look out if you slice your irons! At thirteen, a 252-yard par 4, and again at fifteen, a 169-yard par 3, tee shots must carry a large chasm leading down to the sea. Thirteen's carry is about 125 yards, and fifteen's is about 135 yards. These aren't physically difficult shots, but they are certainly visually intimidating. Adding interest to the course is the commuter train, whose tracks separate the parkland holes from the rest of the course. This also creates one of the difficulties of Stonehaven: To get across the chasm that comes into play on thirteen and fifteen, you must walk down the canyon and under the rail bridge, then back up on the other side. Reverse the walk to come back across. This walk on a gravel path, easily a quarter mile or more, caused one member to complain, "It wears the hell out of soft spikes." The only other anomaly at Stonehaven Golf Club is the seventeenth, a 315-yard par 4, whose narrow fairway is so sloped to left as to be unfair. Though the long carries might be difficult for some women, Anne believes the beauty makes it worthwhile. Even with the long walk and the sloping seventeenth, Stonehaven is a wonderful golf course with challenging holes, friendly members, and great views of the North Sea, the town, and Dunnottar Castle. Well worth more than one round.

Starting up toward the Castle Trail there is a little village with what can only be called a village golf course. **Torphins Golf Club** in Torphins (off the A940) may be a village course, but it is worth a stop if you are along this route. A nine-hole course at 2342 yards and a par 32, Torphins has what many of the village courses lack: a nine-hole price. Too many small course have fees for only a full round (eighteen holes) or an all-day price. We had time to stop for nine holes, and it was economical to just pay for nine holes, especially as good as these. Built in 1896, Torphins is a classic inland design with some elevation changes, but nothing too drastic. The first few holes play up a knock, the middle holes play back and forth across the top of the hill, and the finishing holes, especially the ninth, play down. The third, *Reservoir*, a 291-yard par 4, requires a shot to the foot of a steep rise. The second shot is a blind pitch to the green on top of the rise. The most dramatic hole is *Bettie*, a 359-yard par 4 that starts with a shot off the top of a steep cliff. Tee it high and let it fly, then watch the wind stop the ball and drop it to the fairway. The green is easily approachable but protected by four bunkers. Stop at the pleasant clubhouse/tearoom after your round.

After winding north from the Aberdeen area through the Castle Trail you arrive in the heart of the Whisky Trail at Dufftown. About a half mile northwest of town on B9009 you'll find the **Dufftown Golf Club**. This old (1896), well-conditioned, parkland eighteen-hole track plays uphill, downhill, sidehill, but rarely ever flat. The elevation changes are the main features of the course, and all the defense it needs. Dufftown has some very interesting holes that will challenge every level of golfer. Number two, *Dykeheads*, is a 159-yard par 3 which played well over three clubs longer because of the steep uphill and the stiff, opposing wind. *Fittie Burn* has the distinction of being one of the shortest holes on a regulation course in Scotland. It plays 67 yards from the visitor's tee and only 103 yards from the medals tee. The chip or pitch must cross a deep chasm and stay out of the trees right and left. Also of note is the ninth tee which is one of the highest in the UK at 1294 feet (the clubhouse is at 795 feet). Then comes the tenth hole, which is a 462-yard par 4, with a tee box at 1213 feet elevation and a 339-foot vertical drop to the green. Even for a relatively short hitter it's a drive and a short iron. Another hole which will make an average hitter feel powerful is the 397-yard fourteenth. Downhill and downwind makes this par four almost drivable. One note about Dufftown: Keep your ball to the left here because most holes play with a left-to-right slope.

Once through the Castle Trail and the Whisky trail you arrive at the Moray Firth. All along the Firth are excellent courses, both seaside and parkland. The farthest east of the courses which we've played is at the town of Macduff, next to Banff. Here you'll find another spectacular headland or cliffside course—**Royal Tarlair Golf Club**. Described by some as a clifftop parkland course, it plays along the firth, with great views everywhere. The course was completed in 1923 and received a Royal charter in 1926. Anne notes that Royal Tarlair doesn't boast the canyons of Stonehaven nor the railroad bridge separating part of the course, but then neither does it have the long walks of Stonehaven. It does feature a variety of interesting holes. Number five, *Plateau*, is a 292-yard par 4 with a straightforward uphill tee shot and a second shot which is blind to the plateau green. The 331-yard par 4 twelfth, called *Marven*, is a strong dogleg left. Here you have to decide how much of the dogleg you're going to cut across, then let fire. Be warned: Three bunkers sit waiting to catch any balls that don't travel about 235 yards, and anything shorter than 210 yards will be in the deep, deep rough. But it is the thirteenth, *Clivet*, which gets most of the accolades at Royal Tarlair , and deservedly so. This 152 yard one-shotter gets called "the best golf hole I have ever played" by many golfers. It is a simple hole — shoot straight downhill to a moderately sized green, naturally protected in front by a steep grass canyon, right and back by cliffs dropping down to the sea. There is some bailout area left. With no winds, the shot can be two clubs less than normal (the downhill effect), or two clubs more than normal into a gale. Simple. I do have another warning for you: Be careful to stay away from the cliff edge. My shot landed about ten feet past the green and I could see that it hadn't rolled over the edge. As I started toward it to chip back to the green, I saw that about five feet past my ball was a straight drop of about 100 feet to the crashing waves below. I stepped away from my ball and reached out with my club to tap the ball closer to the green. Remember, this is vacation golf. Royal Tarlair is fun, beautiful, and inexpensive. Give it a try.

Fourteen miles west along A98, the main Moray Firth road, is the seaside community of Cullen. Known as the original home to Cullen Skink, the wonderful smoked haddock and potato chowder, Cullen is also home to an intriguing seaside golf course. The **Cullen Golf Club**, formed in 1896, is another cliffside course, with great views of Cullen Bay and the Firth. The course is short, only 4610 yards with a par of 62, but fun. You best have a decent short game, and try to pick a windless (Ha!) day if you want to score well. Dotted throughout the course are the Three Kings, beautiful rock outcroppings that come into play on several holes. Short though it may be, quality is evident. Old Tom Morris designed the first nine holes. The view as you walk up the second hole is breathtaking. This 130-yard par 3, called *Farskane*, requires a delicate shot to hold the small green, protected by a ditch behind and out of bounds. Another fun par 3 is the 172-yard sixth hole. Called *Bay View* for obvious reasons, this green is protected all around by high rough. To play the hole well, you must hit a high shot, which is then at the mercy of the wind. Hole seven, at 231 yards, is an impressive par 3. The best views on the course are from this long one-shotter, named *Firth View*. A ditch lurks only four yards behind the green, but I certainly didn't have to worry about hitting into it with my first shot. If you haven't guessed yet, we think the best holes on the course are the ten par threes, and the thirteenth, *Red Craig*, is one of the best. On this 149-yard hole the green is hidden behind a rock. An arrow painted on the rock helps you find the way. The whole course is fun, but the par threes, and the views, are what to come for. When leaving the Cullen Golf Club, be sure to drive through the small village of Portknockie to admire the view of the unusual rock formation known as Fiddle Bow Rock.

About eight miles west of Cullen you'll reach **Strathlene Buckie Golf Course** on A990, just east of the village of Buckie. This links-style course plays along the firth, and features a few strategic bunkers and gorse and heather. The first fourteen holes are enjoyable but not tremendously challenging. That's all right, after all, we're on holiday. The last four are across the road and more interesting. The views of the firth are splendid, and by the time you reach the green at eight, you've walked to the next village. The third is a 369 yard par 4 which doglegs along the sea edge. The elevated green is protected by a grass bunker and heavy gorse. *Cabin*, the 272-yard par 4, requires a tee shot which stays left to avoid a deep gully right. And the seventeenth, called *Gullies*, requires a good drive to carry a large chasm and gorse. Bite off as much as you can, but you're lost if you don't make it. Strathlene isn't necessarily easy (I don't think any links course is), but it is fun golf in a beautiful setting and an easy walk as well.

Fifteen miles further west (A98 to Fochabers and B9104), we discovered more links golf at **Spey Bay Golf Club**. Situated very near the Wildlife Centre and historic Ice House, this Ben Sayers designed course (1907) plays along the shores of Spey Bay and the Firth of Moray. Holes eight, ten, eleven, fourteen, and sixteen play adjacent to the beach, with the tee box at sixteen less than ten yards from the water. Typical of links golf, plenty of gorse, heather, and bunkers make an interesting, but fair round. The 374-yard par 4 third begins with a tee shot which must avoid six bunkers on the right. The closest bunker is at 160 yards, and it's 250 yards to clear the last. If you've found a safe landing area, the shot into the green needs to split two more bunkers protecting the green. The sixth is a fairly short, but demanding, 312-yard par 4. This hole is more about accuracy than length. Your second shot needs to clear a small burn about ten yards in front of the green. No run up shot on this hole. I really enjoyed the 351-yard par 4 eleventh, which begins with a blind tee shot—stay to the right for a better chance to hit the green. Ending up too far left of the aiming post, could mean a blind shot to the green. We struggled through one hole of driving rain and three holes of mist, when we played Spey Bay. Still, the round was enjoyable. One couple, who we met on the tee box of the tricky par 3 eighth, carried a picnic lunch, which they ate as we played through.

Leaving the seaside courses, we sought out the **Elgin Golf Club** (Elgin with a "g" as in "gun"). The course is south of village center, just off A941, and is a fairly flat heathland/parkland track, which has hosted many professional tournaments. In contrast to courses like Cullen, Elgin is 6401 yards and par 69, with eight par 4s over 400 yards in length. A nice par 3 at Elgin is the fourth, *The Birches*, at 155 yards. Your tee shot to the slightly elevated green, must clear the two bunkers fronting the green. The wind, which can swirl between the trees, makes this one-shotter tricky. The eighteenth, a par 4 at 440 yards, is the most difficult hole on the course. After numerous long holes, the course ends with another. The deep green is protected on both sides by bunkers, just waiting for any slightly errant shots. The views of the town of Elgin to the north and the Cairngorm Range to the south, makes Elgin Golf Club a challenging break from the seaside courses.

Anne and I seek out the links courses, possibly because they are so different from what we play in Oregon. So, it's back to the links at **Hopeman Golf Club,** about seven miles west of Elgin. Hopeman is an eighteen-hole links course, playing out to and along the firth. The course is, also, in the flyway of jets training from the Kinloss RAF base. You can either think of the planes and their noise as distraction and a bother, or you can revel in the majesty and power as they make their flights, often not more than 500-feet above the course. We choose the later, and enjoy the experience. Among the great holes at Hopeman, the twelfth, right next to the sea, is the standout. *Prieshach* is a 135-yard par 3 whose first shot drops down to a green, about 50-feet below the tee box. Take one or two less clubs because of the drop. But wait. The prevailing wind is directly at the tee—25-35 MPH the day we played—so, consider taking one or two more clubs. One more club worked for me. The green is protected by bunkers left and right and rough all around. Anne thought Hopeman was going to be too easy, but the further we progressed, the more challenging it was. The comfortable clubhouse is a welcome stop after your round, and known for good value meals.

Walker Cup host in 1999, Nairn Golf Club is one of the finest and most well-known of the links courses in this part of Scotland. Sadly, it is one of the most expensive as well. But only a short distance away (across town) is the second of Nairn's great courses, the **Nairn Dunbar Golf Club**. At less than half the price, this combination parkland and links course will provide plenty of challenge. The course opened in 1899 and today plays to a championship length of 6765 yards. Thick gorse, woodlands, and large greens will keep players thinking their way around. The tenth hole, *Westward Ho*, a 411-yard par 4, is considered the toughest. Trees, gorse, and water all come into play. Your tee shot must carry a burn (at over 200 yards), while avoiding the additional challenge of out of bounds. If you negotiate a good tee shot, you're left with a long iron or fairway metal to the green. Nairn Golf Club (the one a mile away) should be on everybody's list of great Scottish courses, but Nairn Dunbar should not be passed by.

Many more courses adorn this stretch of Scotland's coastline—Duff House Royal, Forres, Fraserburgh, Moray Old, and Peterhead Old, to name a few. There are many inland course to choose from as well, such as Ballater, Braemer, and Huntly. It is easy to find excellent golf all throughout the northeast of Scotland. It's easy, too, to find good food and fun non-golf attractions.

PUBS

As we toured the area along the northeast coast of Scotland and the interior region, we found some of the best eating places we've had on our trips. We found the good combination of enjoyable pubs and exciting food, sometimes in the same place. We start this section with a pub which is really out-of-the-way. Catterline is a very small fishing village about three miles south of Stonehaven along A92, and then a half mile down a single track road. How small is it? he asked, sizing up the query. So small that when we asked where the village was, a local told us that when we had passed the four houses and the schoolhouse to get to the pub, that we'd driven through the village. Regardless of the size, at the end of the village is one of the most fantastic pub/restaurants you can imagine—**The Creel Inn**. This is a hunter/fishermen's lodge with booth seating along the walls. The semi-hurricane lamps adequately light the walls, decorated with local seascape art, old photos, and brass ship accents. One room has a small bar with four stools at one end and restaurant seating at the other. A second room serves as a more formal dining area. The full restaurant menu is available throughout. The food is why travelers come to The Creel Inn, a favorite spot of Aberdeen. When we visited, both the lounge and restaurant were packed, and it was a Monday night. The main menu changes seasonally to reflect local products, but a nightly chalkboard is loaded with specials. Several dishes are prepared with crab caught right in the bay—crab soup, garlic crab claws, oven-baked crab. The smoked salmon, locally caught lobster, and cream cheese terrine, served with a citrus mayo, was particularly mouthwatering. We had been told at our B&B to try the great garlic bread, which was toast and half a roast garlic with bruschetta. The entrees (oven baked crab and herb crusted haddock) came with an unusual side dish: butter beans, raisins, and red cabbage. The Creel Inn is a delicious stop and a reason to stay in the area. In fact, two days later we saw a BBC Scotland feature on the restaurant.

At Aberdeen a traveler can choose one of several directions, each leading to a different kind of trip. You can continue north on A90 to Cruden Bay, Petersburgh and Fraserburgh for the seaside experience. Or you can head inland to the Castle and Whisky Trails as we've done. In the heart of the hilly countryside of Strathbogie, full of farms and forests, is Huntly, under an hour from Aberdeen and an hour and a half from Inverness. This former seat of the Gordons is a wonderful location to base an exploration of the Castle and Malt Whisky Trails. If you are stopping at Huntly, we suggest stopping at the **Gordon Arms Hotel** at least for a pint and a meal, if not for lodging. Located in the heart of town, this hotel retains many of its Victorian features. It has a lounge bar which serves meals, a restaurant, the Cheers Bar in an adjoining building, and a function room, which you might want if you're touring with 200 or so of your good golfing buddies. The lounge serves both lunches and dinners and has special menus for children and seniors. We ate in the restaurant so we could watch the main street from a window table. Fine local art adorns the walls of both the lounge and the restaurant. Three of us had dinner, shared a bottle of wine, and shared a Sticky Toffee Pudding for about 11GBP each. On a stormy night (or any night), this is a cozy spot for a meal.

As we continue north we reach the Moray Firth at Banff and Macduff. From here it's only fourteen miles west to the village of Cullen and two interesting eating establishments. Starting with the most rustic, we suggest a stop at the **Three Kings Inn,** just up from the shore on the main road. This old-style public house, with dark walls and beam ceilings, is the stereotypical Scottish pub. At the Three Kings Inn you won't find anything fancy, but you will find it friendly. The Three Kings Inn was turned into a pub in the 1960s, after the old public house was forced to shut down, but you wouldn't know it was that young to look at it. With rock wall interiors and walls decorated with pictures of the owners and the current pub dogs (two cute, friendly Scottie terriers), the Three Kings feels old. The night we visited, we were the only tourists in the pub, but the locals and barkeep were all very friendly as we chatted about our trip and golf. The menu isn't the most interesting, since this is a drinking pub where food is an afterthought. The usual pub items were available for lunch or evening meals. Prices were very low, and a notice said that they didn't accept credit cards to help keep prices low. Two unusual decorations kept our attention as we drank our pint. The top of the front inside wall is lined with cut off ties. "This is not a formal place," said the barkeep. She pointed at one fancy tie and said, "I shouldn't have cut that one; he was really pissed!" Also, the edges of ceiling beams were written on to commemorate special occasions. One said, "Frank R. 5/11/01 – 1/2 century." And another, "Burt's 80th 2/2/2000, Reserved for Burt's 90th." Hope he makes it.

Just across town is a very different dining experience. Not very pub-like, but since the bar is one of the main attractions, we thought we should include **The Seafield Arms Hotel and Restaraunt** (just up from the arch). The restaurant here can only be described as upscale, refined, or elegant. The bar features low tables surrounded by stuffed chairs, and the walls are decorated with great sea paintings, mirrors, and specialty plates. But the bar selection is the real feature at Seafield. Although Seafield has only a typical selection of beers and ales, it offers over 100 single malt whiskies, including an extensive Connoisseur's Collection. It was a real joy selecting a couple of whiskies I hadn't had the opportunity to try. Service is very Continental. We ordered dinner in the bar, and then were taken to our table in the dining room when the meal was ready. The food was superb. We dined on Caesar salad with fresh anchovies, venison pie, and Cullen Skink in Cullen. Although very pleasant, the dining room, with American pop music playing in the background, did lack the same character as the bar. Prices for whisky and our meals were not much higher than normal pub prices and the quality was outstanding. Two very different eating experiences in this town of Cullen on the Moray Firth.

Also along the Moray Firth is the coastal community of Findhorn, set along Findhorn Bay about three miles from Forres (along A96). At the recommendation of the B&B in Forres, we drove to Findhorn to eat at the **Kimberley Inn**. Directly across the road from the bay, where the boats rested on the muddy bottom at low tide, is the Kimberley Inn. Our B&B hostess, Hilda, had described Kimberley Inn as "rustic," and she was right. Dark, wood-paneled walls with a covered bar and six stools is what you see upon entering. A small eating area is to the right, with tables and with a view of the bay. Near the bar are smaller tables and a real fireplace. The entire room is decorated with old photos and prints of World War II planes. An impressive collection of character mugs is shelved over the bar. The food is the star here, not the decor. You can order the usual pub fare, but you'll be better off ordering from a strong selection of specials. We enjoyed a fantastic seafood chowder full of different fish and spiced with a hint of dill. We also had fresh langoustines, right out of Findhorn Bay. I'd like to say they were so fresh that they were trying to crawl off the plate, but I can't because they were very well cooked. One of the interesting features here was that the chef

I stop for an early morning picture of the imposing baronial-style Fyvie Castle.

The eighth at Hopeman, a 346-yarder called Heathery, has a stone wall, as well as bunkers, to protect the green.

Speyside Cooperage is a must stop for anyone interested in the whisky industry. Here is where they put together the barrels used to age the Water of Life.

From the first tee at Stonehaven you can see the eighteenth green, and the ruins of St. Mary's Church behind.

Anne reads the small pub menu at The Three Kings Inn, a friendly pub in the village of Cullen.

Also in the village of Cullen, a better bet for fine dining, is the Seafield Hotel and Restaurant known for its extensive collection of single malt whiskies.

Clivet, the 152-yard thirteenth at Royal Tarlair has the green backed by steep drops to the North Sea.

The twelfth at Hopeman is a breathtaking hole--a fifty foot drop over gorse to a bunker protected green.

served our meal to us and came back later to check on how things were. It was a classy touch. A mix of locals and tourists kept the place busy on the Wednesday we visited, with many of the tourists looking like they were enjoying an extended stay. It really is out of the way to find the Kimberley Inn, but well worth the trouble.

The pubs and restaurants we visited along this area of Scotland are some of the best we've found in the country. They were entertaining, served quality meals, and offered some different dining experiences.

ATTRACTIONS

This area of Scotland is dominated by castles and distilleries, with a few antiquities scattered about. Starting in Stonehaven, we suggest a visit to Dunnottar Castle, visible from the golf course. Spectacular. Breathtaking. Magnificent. Fantastic. These are all descriptors of **Dunnottar Castle**. The ruins are set impressively on a promontory, with cliffs on three sides. The present structures date from the late 14th Century, but indications are that the site held a fortification as early as the 9th Century. Captured by both William Wallace (Braveheart) and Cromwell, there's much history here. The Gatehouse, L-shaped Keep, and newer Waterton's Lodge are some of the buildings available to the visitor, but only after the short hike to the point and the climb down and back up. The castle is not a place to take young children. As interesting as the close-up views are, the vistas, both of the promontory and from the castle, are the real treat. This dramatic ruin is one you might recognize as the setting for Zeffirelli's Hamlet. Bring lots of film when you explore Dunnottar.

On a side road about one mile west of Inverurie lies **Easter Aquhorthies Stone Circle**. A relic of the farming culture that came to the area more than 5000 years ago, Aquhorthies is a classic recumbent stone circle, defined by a large stone that is set horizontally on its edge on the far side of the circle. This recumbent stone (a different type of stone than the rest) is positioned between the tallest of eleven upright stones. Archeologists believe that the circle may have been used to observe the moon. The walk back to the parking lot (about 200 yards) from the circle provides a nice chance to think about the lives of the ancient people who made the circle, their beliefs and activities. Stopping at some of these archeological sites can have a profound affect on your whole trip.

Another experience that may profoundly affect your whole trip, is a stop along Scotland's **Malt Whisky Trail**. *Uisge Beatha*, the Water of Life, Scotch Whisky, is an integral part of Scottish life and culture. In the heart of the Grampian Highlands, between Aberdeen on the east, the Moray Firth on the north, the River Spey on the west, and the River Don on the south, resides much of Scotland's Malt Whisky production. Particularly, the Trail consists of seven distilleries and one cooperage (barrel-making factory), all with visitor's centres. The distilleries (from south to north) of Glenlivit, Glenfarclas, Glenfiddich, Cardhu, Glen Grant, Strathisla, Dallas Dhu, and Benromach are similar, and yet each is unique. It would make a fun trip to visit them all, especially considering that a dram of the good stuff awaits at the end of a tour. But most people don't have that kind of time (or constitution). We have visited several of the distilleries and found the tours informative and enjoyable. At Glen Grant in Rothes we begged off the tour (having just toured Glenfarclas), and instead enjoyed a private tasting conducted by Tom, a long-time distillery employee. Over a dram of Glen Grant whisky we heard about the history of the distillery and received some hints about how to properly taste—in particular, why to add a drop of water to the whisky. We learned that even a drop of water can enhance the flavor of some single malts. At Benromach in Forres, two American golfers from New England and Anne and I were guided on a tour by the distillery manager. We've had good tour guides before, but none with the manager's knowledge. That's a tour I'll always remember—talking golf with the other visitors and whisky with stillman (distillery manager). And it was a very generous pour at the end of the tour. Besides a distillery or two (or three or four), you should save time to tour the Speyside Cooperage in Craigellachie. It's fascinating to watch masters and apprentices building or rebuilding the casks that will later be filled with whisky (single malt whisky must be held in casks for a minimum of three years, and more likely, eight to ten years before bottling.) The audiovisual program was informative, but actually watching the work from the viewing gallery was more instructional. The Malt Whisky Trail winds through some of the most beautiful countryside. The only problem with this part of the trip is that we haven't yet left enough time to play golf at places like Huntly, Keith, and Rothes, all of which have fine courses. Oh well, that's a reason to come back to this area.

Another reason to revisit this northeast section of Scotland is for the **Castle Trail**. The Grampian region is home to numerous castles and great houses, which are grouped under the umbrella (Or should I say "brolly"?) of Scotland's Castle Trail. Dunnottar is one of those castles, but there are other dramatic ruins on this Trail. Tolquohon Castle near Oldmeldrum, Kildrummy Castle near Rhynie, and Balvenie Castle in Dufftown are all worth visiting. My favorite, though, is **Huntly Castle** (also called Strathbogie Castle). The ruins of this baronial residence are what remain of what was the Gordons' family seat for the last five centuries. Built in the 1200s, the castle sits on an estate just off the main square of the village of Huntly. The morning we visited the weather was blustery and the tree-lined drive was littered with leaves and downed branches. The attendant at the small Historic Scotland Visitors Centre apologized for not raising the flags (Scotland's flag and Historic Scotland's). She said that after she climbed the top of the castle tower, the wind almost tore the flags from her hands. We found Huntly to be one of the best-annotated ruined castles we had visited with descriptive plaques throughout. Most impressive is the castle frontispiece, called by Lord Lyon, "Probably the most splendid heraldic doorway in the British Isles."

The Castle Trail not only highlights the area's ruined castles, but also showcases many lived-in or restored castles open to the public. Leith Hall, not far from Huntly, Duff House in Banff, and the fairy tale Craigievar Castle near Alford, are interesting to tour. One of the prettiest, though, is **Fyvie Castle,** about a half mile out of Fyvie on A947. The five towers of Fyvie are named for the five families who owned the castle throughout its history: Prestons, Meldrums, Setons, Gordons, and Forbes-Leiths. Begun in the 13th Century, Fyvie is famous for its impressive 17th Century wheel-stair (reported to be the best in Scotland). Typically fine collections of portraits, arms, and tapestries adorn the castle. Since the early part of the 18th Century, the castle grounds and Fyvie Loch have been a designated parkland. While in the village of Fyvie, stop to see the Fyvie Parish Kirk and Kirkyard, which dates from 1178. Between the Castle Trail and the Malt Whisky Trail, it's been hard to find time for golf on our visits. Maybe it's time for the Grampian area to create a Golf Trail.

If you've had enough of touring castles and distilleries, how about some shopping? At the west edge of Fochabers along A98 is **Baxter's Highland Village**. The Baxter's story begins in 1868, when George Baxter opened a small grocery shop in Fochabers. A small jam factory was added in 1914, and then in 1929 the Baxter's famous Royal Game Soup was invented. After four generations, Baxter's is still a family operation. Today, Baxter's Highland Village is comprised of several specialty shops: the George Baxter Cellar (full range of products), Mrs. Baxter's Cookshop (kitchen supplies), The Coat and Swagger (handcrafted Scottish gifts and clothing), the Baxter's at Home (furniture and decorations), and Baxter's Christmas Experience (from October to December, several Christmas specialty shops). Besides the shops, a small museum replicates the grocery store of 100 years ago, and two restaurants. Situated along the River Spey, Baxter's Highland Village makes a nice break from castle touring. Besides, it's a good place to stock up on cheese and bread, getting ready for the next rounds of golf.

GOLF COURSE INFORMATION

Course: **Stonehaven Golf Club**
Style & Length: Seaside, cliff top with some parkland
                    holes, 5128 yds, par 66
Price: 18GBP
Availability: Prefer you book ahead, avoid Saturday
Phone: (01569) 762124
Web: www.stonehavengolfclub.com

Course: **Torphins Golf Club**
Style & Length: Parkland, 2369 yds, par 32
Price: 12GBP/18, 9-hole price also
Availability: Easy to get on
Phone: (01339) 882115

Course: **Dufftown Golf Club**
Style & Length: Parkland hilly, 5308 yds, par 67
Price: 10GBP
Availability: Easy to get on
Phone: (01340) 820325
Web: www.speyside.moray.org/
                    Dufftown/golf club

Course: **Royal Tarlair Golf Club**
Style & Length: Seaside, cliff top, 5866 yds, par 71
Price: 15GBP
Availability: No restrictions
Phone: (01261) 832897
Web: www.royaltarlair.co.uk

Course: **Cullen Golf Course**
Style & Length: Links, 4610 yds, par 63
Price: 15GBP
Availability: No restriction, busy in heart of summer
Phone: (01542) 840685
Web: www.cullen-golf-club.co.uk

Course: **Strathlene Buckie Golf Club**
Style & Length: Links, 5977 yds, par 69
Price: 14GBP
Availability: Easy to get on
Phone: (01542) 831798

Course:	**Spey Bay Golf Club**
Style & Length:	Links, 6230 yds, par 70
Price:	30GBP
Availability:	Fairly easy to get on
Phone:	(01343) 820424
Web:	www.speybay.com/GOLF

Course:	**Elgin Golf Club**
Style & Length:	Parkland, 6411 yds, par 69
Price:	30GBP
Availability:	Contact in advance, weekends only by arrangement
Phone:	(01343) 542338
Web:	www.elgingolfclub.co.uk

Course:	**Hopeman Golf Club**
Style & Length:	Links, 5590 yds, par 67
Price:	13GBP
Availability:	Can be busy, call
Phone:	(01343) 830578
Web:	www.hopeman-golf-club.co.uk

Course:	**Nairn Dunbar Golf Club**
Style & Length:	Links, 6765 yds, par 72
Price:	40GBP
Availability:	Fairly easy weekdays, weekend restricted
Phone:	(01667) 452741
Web:	www.nairndunbar.com

Chapter Six:
Fife

Golf: Lundin, Lundin Link Ladies, Anstruther, Crail (Balcomie and Craighead), Kinghorn, Burntisland, Balbirnie Park, Dunfermline, St. Andrews (Eden and Strathtyrum)

Pubs: Ship Tavern, Dreel Inn, Kinneuchar Inn, Drouthy Neebors, 1 Golf Place, City Hotel, The Royal Arch

Attractions (for when you can't golf): Lochleven Castle, Dunfermline Cathedral, Abernethy Round Tower and Balmerino Abbey, Secret Bunker, St. Andrews (Golf Museum, Castle, Cathedral, and town)

GOLF

If the Fife is anything, it is the home of golf. Golf may not have started here, and we know the oldest organized clubs weren't here. But without question, the spiritual home of golf resides in St. Andrews at the Old Course. So do hefty green fees (not unreasonable, just hefty). And ditto the need to book well, well ahead. St. Andrews is the Holy Grail, Mecca, and Shangri-la to golfers. What it is not is "out of the way." Even if the Old Course is taken out of the equation, fine out-of-the-way golf can still be found in the Fife.

We'll begin our abbreviated tour of the Fife on the southern shore along A917, the main Fife Coastal Tourist Route. A plethora of great golf courses grace this route. The first of these is just east of the town of Leven (home to a much-respected eighteen-hole course). In the community of Lundin Links are two worthwhile courses, an eighteen-hole and the other a nine. The eighteen-hole **Lundin Golf Club** is a links course which shares a history and the linksland with Leven Golf Club. The two clubs separated in 1868, and the current Lundin course was laid out by James Braid in 1908. The course is mostly links with some parkland features. The fairways are generous, but you can easily lose a ball in the rough. Some very strategic fairway bunkering is found throughout the course. One of the problems I had with the course is that tee boxes are often directly behind the previous green. That gives new meaning to the term "target golf." Lundin is a used as a qualifying course for the British Open, and has some very memorable holes. Number three is a demanding 331-yard two-shotter which plays along the shore of the Firth of Forth. A good drive is needed to avoid the five fairway bunkers, and an equally effective second shot is needed to avoid the four greenside bunkers. *Thorn Tree*, the 352-yard tenth, begins with a drive over gorse to a fairway shared with the eleventh. The second shot here needs to negotiate seven bunkers including, a donut-shaped large bunker fronting the green. What makes this shot even more difficult is that golfers teeing off on eleven are coming at you, and you are hitting toward them. Two good shots are needed to set up a third into a green hidden in the pocket of tall trees at the 499-yard par 5 thirteenth. Trees, an OB right, and a steep slope left make the shots more challenging. No bunkers are needed on this hole. Lundin GC is a popular eighteen-hole course, but just down the road is the too-often-passed-over, nine-hole **Lundin Ladies Course**. It is the oldest exclusively ladies' club, but men can play the course, too, even without a lady. The club was formed in 1890, and at that time men could become Associate Members but could only play with an accompanying lady. In 1909, the present course was laid out by famous architect James Braid to provide a greater challenge for the ladies. The course was closed during World War II, as men were stationed in the clubhouse and much of the course was used as a Victory Garden, a community effort to grow food for the war effort. After the war, the course was gradually returned to playable condition and is today much as it was then. There are some challenging holes at Lundin Ladies, but the number two, a 240-yard par 4, is most memorable. The tee shot on this short, straightforward hole must clear three dramatic 4000 year old standing stones. The thirteen-foot-high stones, believed to be burial markers, standing in the middle of the fairway about 120 to 130 yards from the tee have a tremendous visual impact on that first shot. Bounce your ball off them or nestle the ball up against them, and the impact is much more than visual. Another quality hole is the 133-yard par 3 sixth. From an elevated tee, the hole plays down to a green, protected left and right by bunkers and a two-foot-tall dyke about ten feet in front. The hole plays longer because of the incessant, facing wind. On the Sunday we played, the course was busy, but we weren't pushed and never waited. This is definitely a fun course, especially if you can link it with the next short course.

Twelve miles east, on the main coast road, is the fishing village of Anstruther, home to the Scottish Fisheries Museum. With a small, busy harbor, harbor walk, and seaside shops, Anstruther is worth a stop on any trip. It is also home to an exciting links course set along the Firth of Forth, **Anstruther Golf Club**. Easy to find by following the beach signs, this 1890 Tom Morris-designed course provides some of the most challenging par 3s you'll ever want to play. The course starts out with simple, straightforward holes, with some interesting bunkering. Near the green on the second hole is a large monument to parish men who died in World War I. Many communities have such monuments, and many are incorporated on or near local golf courses. The holes really get exciting starting at number four, a 303-yard par 4 which runs along the cliffs overlooking the Firth of Forth. On a stormy day the wind blows hard onshore, creating the daunting task of aiming over the cliff in hopes that the wind will blow the ball back. On the crisp, clear day we played, the wind was pushing the ball over the cliff and it was difficult to aim far enough left. But it's the fifth, a 235-yard par 3, that I will always remember and want to play again. As if 235 yards isn't enough of a challenge for a par three, your tee shot must try to find a green hidden by thirty-foot embankments on the right and protected by the sea on the left. If you want to lay up (a concept most of us are not used to applying to par 3s), the fairway is barely visible and slopes toward the sea. I honestly couldn't figure out how the locals would play this hole every day (without donating a dozen or so balls to Neptune), but the hole is so beautiful I'd like to find out. Number five at Anstruther really makes sense of the advice one golfing Scot gave: *Ne'er glower at a fower.* (Never glower at a four.) Very true on this hole. The next hole, the 150-yard, par 3 sixth, from the members tees plays from just past the fifth green. The medal (competition) tee is a dramatic climb back up the cliff to where the tee box of the fourth is located — take a look at the shot while you're on the fourth tee. From either tee, your shot must find a green which sits on a shelf with heavy rough all around. The fifth here is probably the hardest par three I've ever seen, and the three holes (four, five, and six) together make a great set. Anstruther is a course that Anne finds exciting, with its varied terrain and susceptibility to the weather.

Traveling a further four miles east, we come to the most easterly tip of the Fife and the typically quaint East Neuk fishing village of Crail. *East Neuk* is the name for the coastal area south from St. Andrews to Largo Bay. Crail is well-known for Crail Pottery, and equally known for its two beautiful links golf courses. **The Crail Golfing Society**, organized in 1786 and the seventh oldest club in the world, maintains two picturesque seaside courses, Balcomie Links and the Craighead Links, both of which provide views of the Firth of Forth, the North Sea, and the Firth of Tay. The older course, **Balcomie Links**, was laid out by Old Tom Morris in 1899, and his signature is still evident in his bunkering (some of the bunkers are terrifying) and long par threes. This course is the shorter of the two at Crail, but the wrong wind can make it play considerably longer. And I don't care when you go, the wind will always be wrong. The first hole takes you down to the sea, and two through five play along the water's edge. Some of the most beautiful holes in the Fife, (or in golf, for that matter), are on the Balcomie links. The first, *Boathouse*, is a good start to the round, with an elevated tee to a green that sports a small dyke in front. It is the fifth, *Hell's Hole*, a 459-yard, par 4 brute, which demands the most attention. The hole, a little like Pebble Beach's eighteenth, skirts along the shoreline, demanding straight shots and lots of nerve to cut off the dogleg to the green, guarded by two bunkers. The last four holes create almost a mini-course. After fourteen you must leave the sea course and climb up to a plateau, upon which the last four play back to the modern clubhouse. Number sixteen is very challenging. A 163-yard par 3, S*pion Kop* calls for a severely uphill tee shot over heavy gorse, with a bunker in the bailout area. The architect may have been prejudiced when he said of Balcomie, "There is not a better course in Scotland." I haven't played them all, but after seeing Balcomie, I don't think I'd argue the point with Old Tom Morris.

As strong as Balcomie is, the course next door is, if anything, more challenging. **Craighead Links** is the newest of the Crail courses, having been designed by Pennsylvanian Gil Hanse in 1995, and opened to the public in 1999. We first played Craighead in 2001 and, without knowing the history, could have easily guessed that the course was a hundred years old. Though the sea doesn't come into play as much as on Balcomie, it is visible from almost every hole, and its influence is felt on almost every shot. This is the course where Anne finally felt successful with the pitch-and-run shot, so necessary in links golf. For beauty, it's hard to match Craighead's 166-yard par 3 seventh, *Kilmonan*. The first offers a lovely downhill shot, with the North Sea breaking just behind the green. Another beauty of a hole is the testing 346-yard, dogleg left twelfth. Don't use the triangle target you see from the tee box as an aiming point; it's actually an aiming post for a different hole. The green is tucked right near the beach and is guarded by bunkers right. Said one Crail native of the new course, "It's a must play course for someone looking for a challenge." For the ladies, Anne believes that

Craighead is the easier course, though both are fun. Balcomie Links tends to get a fair share of golf tours, but even though Crail is only ten miles from St. Andrews, it's enough off the beaten path to be a great out-of-the-way golfing experience.

West along the Fife, past Anstruther and Lundin Links, more fine links courses await. The first we visit is **Kinghorn Municipal Golf Club** near Kinkardy. This eighteen-hole links course overlooks the village harbor and has magnificent views of the Firth of Forth. The two main conditions of play at Kinghorn are the elevation changes and the wind. There's also the added challenge for some of carrying their clubs, since no buggies or trollies are for hire. The saving grace for those not used to carrying is that the course is short, only 4587 yards. There are, though, some very interesting holes at Kinghorn. The third is a 205 yard par 3 where your downhill tee shot must carry a stone fence in front of the green and avoid the bunker behind. A tough shot in heavy winds that are the norm here. The wind is also very much in the picture at *Lang Whang*, a 433-yard uphill par 4 monster. On the day we played the course, we partnered with Colin, who brings his dog, Star, with him for exercise. Colin said that hardly anybody reaches the green in even three shots when the wind is blowing. He was right. I hit three solid woods, but still had twenty yards to go to reach the green. I felt proud of my bogie. Don't confuse Kinghorn with another Fife course, Kingsbarns, which is between Crail and St. Andrews. Kinghorn is a small village course, loads of fun, and 150GBP less expensive than the famous Kingsbarns.

Less than three miles west along the Fife coastal route A921, is **Burntisland Golf Club**. The golfing society at Burntisland is one of ten clubs established before 1800. The eighteen-hole parkland course was originally designed by Willie Park, Jr., and redesigned in 1887 by James Braid. The venerable course plays along Dodhead, with only a couple of noticeable climbs. The views are spectacular. On a clear day it's easy to see Edinburgh Castle, the Scott Monument, and the Forth Rail Bridge. Since the course sits above the firth, the wind is a major consideration most days. The 56 bunkers add to the challenge, as most around the greens are penal and deep. There are no bad holes at Burntisland, and some great ones. *Crowood*, the 347-yard par 4 ninth, is all downhill except for the last forty yards to an elevated green. Heavy rough threatens the left of the fairway, and trees and OB right. It is the first time I've hit a five wood 300 yards. The next hole is a quirky, 342-yard par 4. The hole starts with a blind tee shot. Stay left of the aiming pole because the fairway slopes significantly right. Your second shot needs to negotiate a steep drop to a green, with bunkers behind. It takes playing the hole a few times to figure out how to finesse both the first and second shots.

The *Bunker from Hell* is located left of the green on the par 3 seventeenth. The tee shot is semi-blind, with only the top of the flag visible on the plateau green. The bunker is so deep that there are still golfers trying to get out—the grounds crew comes out each night to feed them! The finishing hole is a challenging downhill 359-yard par 4, with trees right, OB left, and four bunkers around the green. To add to the challenge, everyone in the clubhouse can watch you play the entire hole. Burntisland GC is well worth visiting again and again.

Turning inland from the firth, the Fife offers worthy parkland golf as well as seaside. In the heart of the Fife at Markinch near Glenrothes is **Balbirnie Golf Club**. This 1984 course designed by Fraser Middleton has a very modern clubhouse and well-stocked pro shop. The course is an eighteen-hole undulating track through stands of mature trees. *Deil's Dub*, the 339-yard par 4, is a sharp dogleg right with three bunkers on the inside of the dogleg. The green is guarded by four more bunkers. The next hole is a great visual challenge. The fourth is 199 yards with a mound right, large bunker left, and the green behind. A visually demanding hole, it plays easier than it looks. The fifteenth is a dogleg left (Is that why its called *Kennels*?) which plays uphill, then down to the green, protected by four bunkers. Very classic design.

Before we come back to St. Andrews, I want to take you now to the northwest edge of the Fife. Dunfermline (meaning "fort by the crooked pool") was the capital of Scotland until the Union of the Crowns in 1603. Today, Dunfermline is a beautiful town with pedestrian malls, gargoyled buildings, and historic structures. Not far out of town (two miles west on A994) is the small village of Crossford, home to the **Dunfermline Golf Club, Pitfirrane** (established in 1887). This attractive eighteen-hole parkland course offers an easy walk, interesting holes, plenty of bunkers, no water, and a most unique clubhouses. The friendly staff at the pro shop across from the clubhouse will get you off to a rousing start. The first hole on this J. R. Stutt 1973 design begins with a blind shot to a wide fairway. The green, protected by bunkers right and left, is set into a grove of mature trees. A very pretty beginning. Number seven, *Carlinthorn*, a 480-yard par 5, also begins with a blind tee shot. The hole doglegs right and climbs up, then down. Your shot to the green must avoid the bunkers left and right fronting the green. For a one-shotter, I liked the sixteenth, *Myrend*. Only 156 yards and all of it downhill, but to a well-protected green with bunkers on both sides, it's visually pretty and exciting as well. This course feels old because of the mature trees and how well the course fits the land—of course, it doesn't hurt that the clubhouse is a 600-year-old Tower House! It is one of the best clubhouses I've seen, beautifully appointed and serving a nice dram as well. The Dunfermline Pitfirrane Course has a couple more claims to fame besides the clubhouse. First, on the fourth fairway you can see traces of the old drovers trail, used to drive cattle between Sterling and Dunfermline in the 1400s. Second, it was two Dunfermline members, John Reid and Robert Lockhart, who emigrated to America and created our first golf club, the St. Andrews Club in Yonkers, New York. In fact, the Dunfermline G. C. still holds a tournament each year, named the Lockhart Medal. Anne really feels that these historical features add an extra dimension to the course. To take a break from the links golf on the Fife, give Dunfermline a try.

We leave the parklands of Dunfermline and head back across the Fife to St. Andrews. St. Andrews is a wonderful town to explore and obviously a great town for golf. Even out-of-the-way golf is found in St. Andrews. The Old Course may be the be-all and end-all for golf tours, but the **St. Andrews Trust Links** has care of six courses. Five of them are links courses; the other is parkland. Five courses are eighteen-hole tracks, and one is a nine. Only one of them is the Old Course. Play the Old Course if that's your pleasure. You can get on by booking ahead individually, by booking with a tour, by entering your name in the daily lottery, or by showing up early to the starter (as a single) and waiting to see if you can join a group. It's not impossible to get on, and the fees are only about $160 US. But if that isn't your dream, we suggest that you show up to St. Andrews on a Sunday, when the course is closed to play and becomes a city park for all to enjoy. You can then walk the course at leisure, get your picture taken on the Swilcan Bridge, and go play any of the other interesting Trust courses, like the New Course, Jubilee, Duke's, Eden, Strathtyrum, or Balgove.

Two of the courses that we enjoyed were the Eden and the Strathtyrum. The **Eden Course** is a 1914 Harry S. Colt design, which was updated in 1989. This course is classic links golf without the length or difficulty of the New or Jubilee. Don't get me wrong, it will still test almost every golfer, especially when the elements (wind and weather) traditional to links golf are felt. The course is relatively flat but has plenty of swales, humps, and hollows. Gorse or whin and strategic use of bunkering add to the challenge, as well as out of bounds on several holes. The second hole, a 449-yard par 4, has eleven bunkers, which add to the difficulty of this long two-shotter. The series of five bunkers, starting at about 200 yards out on the left side of the fairway, means you must stay right. After the tee shot the second will seem easy with only one bunker around the green. A narrow landing area is the trouble on the 350-yard par 4 fourteenth— that and not running the ball too far on the fast fairways. For those too far left or too long (250 yards), a large pond awaits. The pond, an unusual feature on a links course, is in play on the second shot, as well, as you try to reach the smallish green.

I very much enjoyed the eighteenth. This 351-yard par 4 played down-wind the day we challenged it. My shot was past the two fairway bunkers on the left, which left me a much easier shot to the green, protected by gorse right and bunkers left. This is quality St. Andrews' golf, especially considering that the price was only $37 US, and the Old Course was the next fairway over.

If the Eden Course is too busy, or you want a second course, try the **Strathtyrum Course,** which plays from the classy Eden Clubhouse and costs about $25 US. Strathtyrum is an eighteen-hole course designed in 1993 by Donald Steel, who was also responsible for revisions to the Eden Course. This is the easiest of the Links Trust eighteen-hole courses, but is still worthy of a round. Strathtyrum is a links course where the hazards are natural rough (enough to lose a ball or two), a few well-placed bunkers, some fairly wild dips and swales on approaches to greens, and narrow fairways made narrower in the ever-present wind. Eleven was a fun par 5. At 447 yards, this short par 5 can be shorter if you can cut the dogleg left (needs a 250-yard drive). Be wary of the bunker right and some severe swales as you approach the green. For a one-shotter, thirteen is a tough hole. It's a tough green to hold, especially downwind, if you clear the two bunkers fronting the green. If you miss, gorse and heather are lurking all around to snag your ball. When we played Strathtyrum, we did so in under three hours—of course, it helped that the Dunhill Cup was being contested on the Old Course, and everyone was there watching.

These courses barely scratch the surface of the golf available in the Fife. Links and parkland jewels abound, and you don't have pay a king's ransom like you would at Kingsbarns.

PUBS

Besides great golf and scenery, the Fife has some entertaining pubs to visit. The seven we've selected to highlight are indeed diverse. They range from harbor side to city center, from college to golf pubs, and from quaint to funky to upscale.

Our first suggestion is to visit the **Ship Tavern** in Anstruther. This harborside pub was built in the 17th Century, but the barkeep said, "It's only been a tavern for the past couple of hundred years or so." No history here. Two sections comprise the tavern. In the front is a small, beautiful, old wood bar with about six-backed stools, while at the very front is a very comfortable booth with a large window and view of the harbor. Decorations throughout the tavern are, of course, nautical, but not overdone. The second room is a larger, nondescript eating section in the back. Eat in the front booth or at the bar like we did. The day we stopped in was absolutely beautiful. The front door was open to the street, and locals would say "Hi" to the barkeep as they strolled by. It seemed that everyone knew each other in the pub—a little like "Cheers," where everybody knows your name. Great place to meet locals. The food and beverage selection was fairly limited: six taps, a few malts, mostly variations of fish and chips. This is a friendly place to stop for pint, dram, or quick bite, or to enjoy a great view.

A second suggestion for Anstruther, which doesn't have the harbor view but does have more history and ambiance, is the **Dreel Tavern** in the middle of town on the main Fife coastal road. The tavern is an old 1600s coaching inn, very traditional in design and decor. The walls are covered with old photographs, and dining areas are lighted by hurricane lamps. Stone walls and a real fireplace give Dreel a warm, rustic feeling. It offers an enticing menu with numerous specials, and a full service bar for guests. In the nonsmoking section (the conservatory), we shared a scallop and prawn starter that was delicious. Plan to book ahead, even on a week night, or be prepared to wait, since the Dreel Tavern is deservedly well-known and very busy.

In the same area there's a spot that exudes the feel of small village pubs. Just a mile inland from Elie, on B941 in the Village of Kilconquhar, is the **Kinneuchar Inn**. Interestingly, "kinneuchar" is the phonetic pronunciation of "conquhar." The village is sparse, except for a picturesque church and a few shops. The village basically serves some of the needs of the nearby Kilconquhar Castle Resort. The inn, though, serves the needs of the local population. When we stopped after a round at Lundin GC, we were the only visitors in the place. A small pub section, and an equally small dining room, comprise the pub. Staff, patrons and their dogs were friendly and the meals decent. Kinneuchar Inn would be the kind of place in which you get very comfortable very quickly.

From Anstruther and Kilconquhar we head north to St. Andrews for the next two pubs. These two are within a five-minute walk of each other, but are very different in style. The first pub, **Drouthy Neebors** (meaning "thirsty neighbors"), is part of a chain with others in Dundee, Sterling, Edinburgh, Glasgow, and Ayr. It's a neighborhood pub, and the neighborhood is St. Andrews University. Located on South Street just a couple of doors down from the West Port, the old city gate, Drouthy Neebors is a meeting place for locals, a drop-in spot for students, and relaxing place to quaff a draught, and sip some leek and tattie soup, or munch a toastie (a toasted sandwich). The St. Andrews incarnation is dark, with a row of small tables in the front and more spacious seating in back. We chose a table by the front window so we could watch

The 11th Century Round Tower lies in the heart of the small village of Abernethy on the Fife. Keys are available in the bakery across the road.

St. Andrews Cathedral ruins are full of beauty and history.

The memorial to, and graves of, Young and Old Tom Morris rests at the side of St. Andrews Cathedral graveyard.

The shared green for the fourteenth and eighth holes at Burntisland Golf Club affords spectacular views across the Firth of Forth to the capital city of Edinburgh.

We've seen many ancient stones on Scottish golf courses, but none are more impressive than the seventeen-foot-tall stones on the second hole at the Lundin Ladies course.

The Ship Tavern on the harbor of Anstruther is a quaint spot for a pint and a bite of lunch.

Blacklaw, an ancient volcanic plug, is visible when looking back toward the tee on the thirteenth hole at Balbirnie Park.

The green on Lang Man's Grave, Crail Craighead's fourteenth hole, is protected by a deep pot bunker and stone wall.

passersby. With a wide selection of ales, beers, and malts, and a complete pub-style menu, including several inexpensive specials, Drouthy Neebors is a neighborly place to drop in on while touring or shopping.

The second pub, **1 Golf Place** (The pub's name is also its address.), is located in The Links Hotel, just down from the Clubhouse of the Royal and Ancient Golf Club of St. Andrews (The R & A). Whereas Drouthy Neebors is college-local, 1 Golf Place is golf-local. Make no mistake, this is a golfers' pub. Booth-back snugs stretch along the outer wall, and a small bar with nine stools accommodates other patrons. The second bar upstairs has an outside balcony for those nice days. And the whole place is decorated with golf photos and memorabilia. 1 Golf Place serves the usual beers, ales, and malts, but sports something we didn't see in other pubs, an espresso machine. It features a complete pub menu and a separate dinner menu with a large selection of salads. Catering to the golf crowd, 1 Golf Place offers sandwiches to go and a selection of breakfast items for those with early tee times. After a round on the Eden Course and browsing in the golf shops, we stopped in here and split a delicious bacon cheese burger, chips and slaw. I know it's not Scottish, but it was wonderful.

It's about 30 miles from St. Andrews to Dunfermline, and it's about that far in atmosphere from 1 Golf Place to **Weaver's Bar and Restaurant in the City Hotel** in Dunfermline. You can enter via the front door and lobby, or walk in the back door to Weaver's (named for one of the area's main industries, textile weaving). Built as a coaching house in 1775, City Hotel has had a long history of serving the public. On the afternoon we stopped, the pub was filled with local shoppers and tourists. This is a modern, bright pub with a divided restaurant section close by. It was fun to walk around the room looking at the history displayed in the old photographs which decorate the walls. The extensive menu is available in the pub, as well as in the restaurant. The food portions were generous and well-prepared. The hotel has a second bar, the Cask Bar, which opens out to the main street and has a smaller pub menu. It's a good place for a pint and a quick bite, but the better food is at Weaver's.

The last of the pubs of the Fife isn't in the Fife. Less than 20 miles north from St. Andrews is the small coastal community of Broughty Ferry (a suburb of Dundee). We've used Broughty Ferry as a convenient base for exploring the Fife, and it's often less expensive than areas like St. Andrews. Numerous B&Bs, small guesthouse hotels, and some very good pubs are found here. In the heart of the shopping district in Broughty Ferry, about three blocks west of Broughty Castle, is **The Royal Arch Lounge and Restaurant**. This art-deco-slash-oriental decorated eatery is a plush choice for a meal. The pub was named for the former use of the building as a masonic lodge. Because of negative attitudes towards Masons in some places, the local lodge adopted the Royal Arch, a landmark of Dundee torn down in 1960. You have a choice of three different pub rooms: a large restaurant, a bar, and a combination. We ate in this latter room with booths along the walls and tables in the middle. The room is decorated with Tiffany-style lamps and some very well done paintings of the local area. The very complete menu includes the usual starters and snacks and two pages of mains. The split pea soup was very tasty, with a hint of chili pepper, and the seafood platter included mussels, mackerel, Arbroath smokies, scampi, crab salad, and smoked haddock. A very impressive platter. Besides the Royal Arch, Broughty Ferry boasts several other interesting places for a pint and a bite. Along the sea front is a Ship Inn, and up the street is the Ferry Inn, with a lively pub downstairs and more elegant dining room upstairs. Broughty Ferry may not be on the Fife, but its a good place to stay as you golf and tour on the Fife.

ATTRACTIONS

Every place you go in the Fife has good golf available, but the weather will not always be conducive to golf. Besides, there is so much to see, especially of historical significance, that you'll want to plan some time for touring. Anyway, that's why you're traveling on your own instead of taking a golf tour like my club was planning: 15 of the hardest, most expensive courses in ten days with all but lunches and one evening meal planned. The self-guided golf tour can be much more rewarding, especially because you can take your time to explore the riches of the Fife.

As in other areas of Scotland, there's so much to see and do in the Fife that we can only pick out a few of the features we liked best. Starting at the west end of the Fife, we first visit a unique historical site, **Lochleven Castle** in Kinross (just off the M90). What makes Lochleven Castle unique isn't that Mary Queen of Scots was imprisoned here, but the ferry ride over to the castle island. They call it a ferry, when actually its a small, half-open passenger boat with an outboard motor. I'm not personally too fond of boat travel, but the only problem with this ten-minute trip is that the only person who gets a life jacket is the boat driver. Now that inspires confidence! Mary wasn't the only notable who visited this 14th century castle—she visited once on her own and then again, not by her own choice. Sir William Wallace, the great patriot of *Braveheart* fame, is thought to have captured the fortified island before 1305. Robert I (Robert the Bruce) used the castle as a state prison in the

1320s. Lochleven is a well-preserved ruin today with the Curtain Wall and Tower House (which may be the oldest in the country) fairly complete. As you stand in what was Mary Queen of Scot's Tower House prison room, you feel not only a chilling sense of the castle's history, but also of Scotland's.

Traveling ten miles south on the M90, we arrive at the old capital city of Dunfermline. This ancient city (one of Scotland's oldest) is dominated by the **Abbey Church** and the **Palace of Dunfermline**. Again we find ourselves in a place of tremendous history and beauty. The nave of the *Old Church*, dedicated in 1147, is the only section still intact, and it's a wonderful huge room. The roof (must be 30 feet tall) and second floor clerestory are supported by eleven massive stone pillars, each of a different design. The room is empty, which adds to the sense of how massive it is. In the New Church can be found the grave of Robert the Bruce (except for his heart, which is in Melrose). The grave is marked by a full-size, beautiful brass slab (1889) of the figure of Bruce, and it is set beneath a splendidly carved pulpit (1890). A brass cast of the skull of Robert the Bruce is also displayed. Gruesome, but interesting. Besides Bruce, at least twenty-two other Royals are interred, dating back to 1093. The Palace of Dunfermline is just across the grounds from the Church and is almost as old, dating to the mid-1100s. The Guesthouse of the Benedictine monastery became the Palace in the 1600s. A tourist office is on the Palace grounds, and the attendant gave us a personal visual tour of the Palace. After eighteen-holes at Dunfermline Pitfirrane, we weren't anxious to clamber up and down the Palace ruins. Lochleven and the church and ruins in Dunfermline are very well-presented by guides and information books. The next sites are not so professionally presented, but that just adds to their charm.

Both the Abernethy Round Tower and the Balmerino Abbey are on the north side of the Fife, off A913 and A92. About eight miles southeast of Perth, at the very edge of the area known as the Fife, is the little village of Abernethy. Like many small villages, there's not much to distinguish Abernethy from the next village. Not much except a round tower. The **Abernethy Round Tower** is an Irish-type, 11th Century tower and is a relic of the early Celtic settlement here. It supposedly is one of only two intact, round towers in Scotland, the other being in Brechin, Angus. The 74-foot tall tower stands at the kirkyard gate, and the key to the tower is available from the bakery across the road. Look for signs of the two distinct periods of construction and Pictish symbol stone at the base. Twelve or so miles further along A92, turn on the unnumbered road directing you to **Balmerino Abbey**. The ruins of this Cistercian abbey, founded in 1229, rest on a hill overlooking the Firth of Tay. We first visited the abbey one stormy day (unfit for golf) in 2001. The National Trust caretaker showed us around the ruins, pointing out several features including Mason Marks (signs left by the masons who cut the stones, which can be seen in many abbeys, cathedrals, and castles) and features of Roman architecture. Both the round Tower and the abbey are interesting stopping points in the Fife and are certainly not as commercialized as some sites.

Near Anstruther, on the Firth of Forth side of the Fife, is one of Scotland's well-kept secret attractions. In fact, it's called **Scotland's Secret Bunker**. On B940 between Anstruther and St. Andrews is a secret Cold War Command Centre, now open to visitors. Here you can wander in the underground nuclear fallout shelter, which would have been used in the event of a nuclear attack on Great Britain for civilian and military survival operations. As someone who grew up with "duck-and-cover" drills in school, I was fascinated with the entire set up. The extremely well-done displays are very informational. We would have spent more time visiting, had we not had a tee time in St. Andrews.

Scotland's Secret Bunker is only ten miles from **St. Andrews**, one of the best tourist towns in Scotland. Of special note to golfers is the **British Golf Museum**. This museum, only a wedge shot from the first tee at the Old Course, houses 500 years of golf history, with photos, videos, and all manner of memorabilia. The sense of history presented here is fascinating; the evolution of clubs and balls is particularly well presented. St. Andrews is a fine shopping town as well, with antique and tourist shops along the two main commercial streets, South Street and Market Street. In one antique shop, we found clubs made by Old Tom Morris and other famous 19th Century club makers. Another shop displayed a vast array of old photos of courses and golfers. Although this is an interesting town for non-golf visitors, it really is a treasure trove for golf shoppers. Some fantastic specialty golf shops are near the Old Course, such as the Old Tom Morris Ltd. Shop, Braur's, and Auchterlonies of St. Andrews.

Aside from golf and shopping, St. Andrews is full of great history. It is home to **St. Andrews University**, Scotland's oldest and most well-known university, and many of its buildings are open to curious tourists. As historical as the University is, it also adds a vibrancy to the town. We happened to be in St. Andrews the weekend before school opened for the new year. The place was a madhouse of activity. The Leuchars Air Show (Britain's largest) was taking place only four miles away, so jets were performing practically over our heads. College students and parents were wandering about, shopping for the new semester. It didn't hurt that the weather was absolutely perfect—70 degrees and windless in the middle of September.

More ancient than the University are both the St. Andrews Castle and Cathedral. The **St. Andrews Castle** was built about 1190, but the existing structure dates from about the 14th Century. The castle sits on a point of land overlooking St. Andrews Bay and the Firth of Tay. A few rooms are open to the visitor, but a much more intriguing part of the castle begs to be explored. The siege of 1546-47 left one of the most interesting pieces of siege engineering extant anywhere in Europe: the mine and countermine. While attacking forces were tunneling beneath the castle walls to try to gain entry, the defenders were counter-mining in order to stop the invaders. Today the mine and countermine can be explored, but the passages are small and often damp. The Castle has an excellent visitors centre with audiovisual information about the history of the castle.

Just a short walk from the castle and along a path that follows the curve of the bay, are the ruins of the great **St. Andrews Cathedral** (begun in 1160) and its predecessor, **St. Rules Church.** St. Andrews Cathedral, when intact, was the largest cathedral in Scotland, and certainly the most powerful. Of St. Rules Church, built in the early 12th Century in much the same design as Dunfermline Abbey, all that remains is the tower. The 157-step climb to the top affords visitors dramatic views over the city and out to the linksland of the St. Andrews Links Trust. The huge east gable, with its twin spires, makes a beautiful picture, when taken through the west doorway. You can wander the grounds of the cathedral for hours and never see all the treasures here. Don't miss the stone slabs housed in the vaulted undercroft in the south cloister range. And, for the golfer, be sure to find the beautiful memorial at the graves of Old and Young Tom Morris in the cathedral graveyard.

St. Andrews is definitely the Queen of the Fife, but the entire area is filled with rich sites for the tourist and wonderful golf for the duffer.

GOLF COURSE INFORMATION

Course: **Lundin Links Golf Club**
Style & Length: Links, 6394 yds, par 71
Price: 40GBP
Availability: Very busy, call
Phone: (01333) 320202
Web: www.lundingolfclub.co.uk

Course: **Lundin Ladies Golf Club**
Style & Length: Lowland, 2365 yds, par 34
Price: 10GBP/day
Availability: Competitions on Wed. and some weekends
Phone: (01333) 320832

Course: **Anstruther Golf Club**
Style & Length: Links, 2266 yds, par 31
Price: 8GBP
Availability: Visitors welcome anytime
Phone: (01333) 310956

Course: **Crail Golfing Society, Balcomie Links**
Style & Length: Links, 5922 yds, par 69
Price: 30GBP
Availability: Restricted 10:00-noon & 2:00-4:00
Phone: (01333) 450868
Web: www.crailgolfingsociety.co.uk

Course: **Crail Golfing Society, Craighead Links**
Style & Length: Links, 6728 yds, par 71
Price: 30GBP
Availability: Restricted 10:00-noon & 2:00-4:00
Phone: (01333) 450868
Web: www.crailgolfingsociety.co.uk

Course: **Kinghorn Golf Club**
Style & Length: Links, 5166 yds, par 65
Price: 12GBP
Availability: Easy to get on
Phone: (01592) 890312
Web: www.kinghorngolfclub.co.uk

Course:	**Burntisland Golf Club**
Style & Length:	Inland, 5965 yds, par 66
Price:	18GBP
Availability:	Busy, call ahead
Phone:	(01592) 874093

Course:	**Balbirnie Park Golf Club**
Style & Length:	Inland, 6212 yds, par 71
Price:	25GBP
Availability:	Can be busy, call
Phone:	(01592) 612095

Course:	**Dunfermline Golf Club, Pitfirrane**
Style & Length:	Parkland, 6121 yds, par 72
Price:	25GBP
Availability:	Visitors welcome except on Saturday
Phone:	(01383) 723534

Course:	**St. Andrews Links, Eden Course**
Style & Length:	Links, 6112 yds, par 70
Price:	25GBP
Availability:	Visitors welcome, check in advance
Phone:	(01334) 477036
Web:	www.standrews.org.uk/courses

Course:	**St. Andrews Links, Strathtyrum Course**
Style & Length:	Links, 5094 yds, par 69
Price:	17GBP
Availability:	Easy to get on
Phone:	(01334) 477036
Web:	www.standrews.org.uk/courses

Chapter Seven:
The Borders and East Lothian around Peebles

Golf: Innerleithen, Peebles, West Linton, St. Boswell, Cardrona, Glencorse, Kilspindie, North Berwick, Hawick

Pubs: Corner House Hotel, Traquair Arms Hotel, Crown Hotel, Park Hotel Bar, Neidpath Inn, Ship Inn, Golden Arms, Horseshoe Inn, Old Aberlady Inn, Old Clubhouse

Attractions (for when you can't golf): Abbeys (Melrose, Jedburgh, Dryburgh), Dawyck Botanic Gardens, Kailzie Gardens Traquair House, Abbotsford, Rosslyn Chapel, Robert Smail's Print Shop.

GOLF

The Borders and East Lothian regions are full of great golf, much of it old and some of it new. Choosing Peebles as a central location for exploring this area makes good sense. It is close to Edinburgh (about 45 minutes) and only a little further from Glasgow (about an hour and a quarter). It's also central to some of the best golf in the area. As a town Peebles makes a great base for exploration, with it has pleasant B&Bs, guesthouses, hotels, restaurants, and shopping. It's a wonderful town to walk the High Street shopping area; the town is bustling with locals every day. This was the first place we stayed on our first trip to Scotland, and it's a town we go back to every year. But Peebles wasn't the first place we played golf. That was Innerleithen.

Innerleithen is a smaller community seven miles east of Peebles on A72. Visitor attractions and interesting eating await in Innerleithen, but on our first day in Scotland in 2000 it was golf we wanted to find. The nine-hole **Innerleithen Golf Club** introduced us to Scottish golf, and our lives haven't been the same since. Innerleithen Golf Club is a pleasing beginning to a Scottish golf experience—it's old, 1886, and it has typical Scottish design features. From the very first hole, we knew we "weren't in Kansas anymore." The first hole, a 177-yard par 3, plays across the second and the fourth fairways, then over the third green; and a burn flows down the middle and fronts the green, and the main road stretches along the right side. A most interesting start to our Scotland golf experiences! The first hole may be the most convoluted, but there are other exciting holes. One of the exciting holes at Innerleithen is *Pirn Craig*, the 433-yard, par 4 third. For the tee shot, you climb up the side of Pirn Craig to a tee box about 25 feet above the fairway. The first shot must then skirt the hillside on its way to a generous fairway below. Cut it too close on the right and the ball will hang up on the hillside rough; aim too far left and you may find your ball (if you can) in the rough defining the left boundary of the hole. The second shot is easier, but the target is the small green that is just below the tee box at one. Freedom of the Fairways, a discount golf promotion, labels this hole "one of the best par 4s in the Borders." Another interesting hole at Innerleithen is the short, 100-yard par 3 fifth, called *Hill*. Aptly named, this one-shotter plays across the road and straight up a hill to a plateau green, about 20 feet above the tee box. The shot is blind; only the top of the flag can be seen from the tee. Miss the green on any side and you're hunting in the tall grass for your ball. It's a fun hole that I have special feelings for since it was my first par in Scotland. Before leaving Innerleithen Golf Club, I would mention the par-5 eighth, called *Dyke*. This was the first time we saw stone fences in play on a golf course; a feature we would find on many other courses. In reflection, Anne thinks of this as typifying a small village course, nestled into a glen, with sheep dotting the hillsides, and a small burn flowing through the middle of the course. Innerleithen also has a small clubhouse, with a lounge/bar open daily from noon to 2:30, with light snacks available.

Back in Peebles a fine undulating (undulating to the Scots; hilly, to us), eighteen-hole parkland course lies at the west end of town. The **Peebles Golf Club**, founded in 1892 and remodeled by Harry Colt in 1934, offers some of the most stunning views in the Borders area. The course climbs into the hills and presents views of the town below, the River Tweed, and the hills surrounding. The views alone are worth a visit, but the golf is excellent as well. The course, renowned for its condition, presents some interesting challenges. Number five, *Meikle Hope* (meaning "big hope"), is a 342-yard par 4 which plays from an elevated tee out toward a right-sloping fairway, protected on the left by a bunker just waiting to grab any shot that is played too high. The second shot must find an elongated green with a bank on the high side and bunkers on the low side. Visually, its a beautiful hole, but it requires two excellent shots to have a chance at par or better. The par 4, 359-yard eighth hole, *Peggy's Lea*, provides the best views of the town and hills and plays to a well-bunkered green. The hole most mentioned after a round is the par 3, 193-yard sixteenth. This medium-length, demanding one-shotter challenges the golfer with out of bounds on the left and back, and a burn fronting the green. You cross the burn on a delightful centenary bridge, similar to the Swilcan Bridge at the *Home Hole* eighteenth at St. Andrews Old Course. If imitation is the sincerest form of flattery, the sixteenth at Peebles does a good job paying tribute to golf history. Anne likes this course and says, that except for the hills, the golf is not too difficult. Before you leave Peebles Golf Club, be sure to stop in for refreshments at the beautiful new clubhouse, dedicated in 1998 by Prince Andrew.

A short 12 miles northwest of Peebles, via A72 and B7059, is the fairly flat moorland tract of **West Linton Golf Club**. This 1890, James Braid-designed, eighteen-hole course is an enjoyable contrast to the hills at Peebles GC. The staff at West Linton have been particularly friendly and accommodating the three times we visited. It is one to which we keep returning. In fact, Carl, at Lindores House in Peebles tells a story about actor Michael Landon who, just before he died from cancer, stayed in the area to play West Linton because he appreciated how they treated him. Several holes stick in our memory. The sixth, *Mendick*, a 360-yard par 4, starts with a slightly downhill tee shot to a well-bunkered fairway, which narrows near the green. Try to stay in the middle, lest trees on both sides encroach on your second shot to the green, also well bunkered. *Woolfe's Wood*, the par 4, 447-yard eighth is the number-one handicap hole, for good reason. A blind tee shot to a fairway which falls away left is a challenging start. The long second shot, through a slight dogleg right, is to a green with heavy rough, and out of bounds right and bunkers left. This hole, for me, plays as a testing par 5 instead of a par 4—it's a good example of a hole which should be played with my own personal par in mind, regardless of what the card says. Following this long par 4 is the difficult *Kittley Knowe* (*knowe* meaning "hillock"), an interesting 162-yard par 3. At the furthest limit of the course, you play to an elevated, forward-sloping green with a large bunker left, and a drop off on all other sides. Anne noted a sense of hugeness of the course here, because we could barely see the clubhouse off in the distance. It's at this point in your round that you may wish the Scots placed more toilets on their courses. Though, between the ninth green and tenth tee there is a convenient (and often used) stand of trees. West Linton has provided some enjoyable memories, outside of the golf itself. During one round, we watched sheep dogs work a flock in the fields adjacent to the fourteenth hole. Scotland offers several places where tourists can find more formal demonstrations of working dogs, but it was a treat to watch them in their everyday work. We have also had good experiences with pairing up with other golfers at West Linton. We've never had a bad experience pairing up in Scotland, and the retired civil servant we played with here in 2000 was a delight. He had a wealth of knowledge of the course and the area, and a memorable way of saying "Oh, no!" to each bad shot I made that day (and there were several). West Linton GC also has a relatively new clubhouse (1997) with snacks available midday to evening most days.

For a shorter round while exploring the sites of the Borders area we'd suggest stopping at **St. Boswell Golf Club,** eight miles southeast of the shopping town of Galashiels (the largest town in the central Borders area). This easy-to-walk nine-hole course was designed by famed golfer/architect Willie Park Jr., from Musselburgh in 1899, for fee of five pounds. The course has an complex history. It was closed during the war years (1944-1947), and when reopened, struggled to stay open, particularly because of heavy damage during the 1948 floods. In 1954 the club folded because of lack of interest. Local golfers, regretting the absence of a home course, rebuilt St. Boswell Golf Club in 1958, trying to maintain as much as possible the original layout. Today, the course is a well-respected, busy parkland tract set along the banks of the River Tweed. There is a small lounge bar, but no pro shop and no trolley rental (but it's an easy course to carry your clubs). The second hole, a 161-yard par 3, is the only non-flat hole on the course. The large green provides a good target for your shot from the elevated tee. Take about one club less than normal for the distance, but keep the shot straight because the green is well guarded by bunkers. I found the ninth, a 256 yard par 4, to be a short, but demanding, test. The tee shot must skirt a large beech tree to reach a shelf fairway and green. It's prudent to lay back on the first shot (150-190 yards), but that means the second shot is half blind, with only the top of the flag visible. It might be tempting to try a long sweeping hook to reach the green, or at least the raised part of the fairway, but that would bring into play heavy rough on the left. A fun hole! Besides pleasurable golf, the course has much else to offer. Grand views of the River Tweed, with fly fishermen trying their luck, are plentiful. Rabbits, ducks, and a profusion of wildflowers (even in September) brightened the whole course. The course even presents an enigma to take your mind off golf. Between the sixth green and seventh tee lurks a small, innocent looking pond with a bridge to cross over. But on this bridge a sign warns, "THIS POND IS DANGEROUS." No information was provided as to why the pond was dangerous. It didn't look particularly deep, or as if it had poisonous water. The rest of the round, I kept conjuring up images of miniature Nessies lurking beneath the lilly pads. St. Boswell Golf Club makes a short, enjoyable stop, especially while wandering through Abbey country.

As a change of pace from courses more than 100 years old, try the **MacDonald Cardrona Hotel Golf and Country Club** between Peebles and Innerleithen on A72. For the next few years we may be able to classify this as an out-of-the-way golf course, but once the resort hotel (which opened in the Spring of 2003) has a few years of operation, you may need to book six month out for your tee time. This is a heathland/parkland course, designed by Dave Thomas who also designed The Belfry, with the look of a links course, complete with rolling fairways and dune-style grasses. It reminded us of what Gleneagles might have looked like early in its history. Fairways are wide, but beyond the first cut of rough the balls are lost (very penal). For me, holes two, three, and four made a fantastic trio. Perhaps the most interesting is number two, a 521-yard par 5, which has eight strategically placed bunkers to catch all but the best shots. It's easy on this hole to play from bunker to bunker to bunker—I know because I did. In contrast is the short, 280-yard par 4 third hole. Bunkers threaten the left side (240 yards to carry uphill), where you really want to be for the second shot. Challenges abound! Even if you are in good position on the first shot, the second shot is mostly blind: you can see the top of the flag, but none of green. The ruins of an abbey or priory are visible in the field behind the green. The final hole in this set is the downhill fourth, a 429-yard par 4. It's a fairly long hole, but the tee shot downhill takes some of the sting out of the length. From the tee, the fairway swings out to the right and doglegs left around a large bunker. A 230 yard drive will carry the bunker and cut significant yards off the second shot, making it a great risk/reward shot. My normal drives carry 200 to 210 yards and I carried the bunker with plenty to spare—okay, by a few feet, but I did carry it. The green is open at the front, but protected by bunkers on both sides. The River Tweed flows along the length of the hole; pretty to look at, but not really in play. Cardrona is one of the few courses where the ninth comes back to the clubhouse, which is housed in a recently renovated rail station; thus, it's possible to play just nine. Anne gives the caution that the couse is not always lady-friendly—short and down the middle can still get you into real trouble. Cardrona is still relatively unknown and inexpensive but, as the crowded tour bus that arrived as we were leaving proved, it won't stay out-of-the-way for long.

North and east from Peebles, we discovered that the Borders hills give way to the East Lothian golf mecca around Muirfield and Gullane. The main route from Peebles toward Edinburgh (A701) goes through

Penicuik and right past the **Glencorse Golf Club**. This is a tight, eighteen-hole par 64 course which is very hilly—not undulating, but mountain goat hilly! It does have, though, some interesting holes which make the climbing up and down worth the effort, at least once. Tight fairways, elevation changes, and 14 burn crossings make Glencorse especially challenging. The pro told us as we headed out that we would need to be particularly accurate with long irons. The signature hole for the club is the fifth, *Forrester's Rest*, a 237-yard par 3. It is a beautiful downhill hole with a burn running about 15 yards in front of the green. Number eleven is a 211-yard par 3 which doglegs around trees and over the burn. Play for the left side of the green, and the wind and the slope can help you. Playing at Glencorse will help you appreciate the openness of some of the East Lothian links courses.

From Penicuik swing east on the coastal route to drive to some really fantastic links courses. To give a sample of the type of golf in this area, we'll mention two courses, one unknown and one almost too well-known for this book. The lesser-known **Kilspindie Golf Club** resides in Aberlady along Firth of Forth, about 20 miles east of Edinburgh. This links course has six holes which play along Gosford Bay, numerous fairway and greenside bunkers, and mildly undulating greens. "I enjoyed every shot," "First class," and "An absolute gem" were typical comments from the players we met in the clubhouse after our round. On the course, number eight, *Gosford Bay*, is a dramatic hole. A par 3 of 162 yards, the tee shot needs to carry 150 yards of the bay to a green, protected by several bunkers. But it isn't the hardest hole. That's the fourth, *The Target*, a 365-yard par 4, where the fairway is a gentle curve to the right around the sea edge. The fairway also slopes to the right toward the beach, which is OB. The green is a small target on a point and surrounded by several bunkers. The final hole is really unforgettable. For men it is 252 yards and plays as a par 4, but for ladies it is 240 yards and plays as a par 3! Anne really screamed about that. From both, tees shots must avoid the stone fence which bisects the fairway. Despite the eighteenth, Anne shot her best score in Scotland, and says the course is fairly easy to read. It may be because the course is only 5480 yards that it doesn't receive more acclaim. Whatever the reason, it's nice to find a gem like this in an area dense with courses.

Far better known is the **North Berwick Golf Club** (pronounced "Bear-ick"; also known as the West Course). This is an Open qualifying venue when the championship is played at Muirfield. The reason I include it here is that, for a "famous" course, it is overshadowed by Muirfield and Gullane #1, it's not too difficult to get a game, and it is relatively inexpensive, at only 42GBP (2004 prices). And, most importantly, it is a world class course with one of the most famous holes in golf.

First built in 1832 as a nine hole course, then expanded to eighteen holes in 1877, and finally redesigned into the present configuration by Ben Sayers in 1932, North Berwick West is a venerable club, thirteenth oldest in the world. Pay at the fully stocked pro shop (which is almost buried in the first fairway), and check in at the starters shack. The first hole makes an exciting start to the round. A 328-yard par 4, *Point Garry* begins by encouraging a 190-yard lay-up to the bottom of a steep rough-covered hill. You can be thankful none of North Berwick's more than 100 bunkers are around the first green, because the shot to the green is blind. Thirteen, *The Pit*, requires an imaginative approach to a sunken green, hidden behind a stone wall which runs diagonally to the fairway. It's a hole you have to see to understand. The famous hole at North Berwick is the 192-yard par 3, called *Redan*. The best description of this hole was given by famous golf writer Bernard Darwin, who said Redan is "a beautiful one shot hole atop a plateau with a bunker short of the green, to the left, and another further on to the right, and we must vary our mode of attack according to the wind, playing a shot to come in from the right or making a direct frontal assault." *Redan* is one of the most copied golf holes in the world. It's a daunting hole which I wish I had played better. Like Royal Dornoch or Macrihanish, North Berwick West is how links golf should be.

Lastly, on our way south from Peebles (before we get to the next chapter) we find interesting golf at Hawick (pronounced "Hoik"). About two miles from the center of the village, known for its woolen mills, is **Hawick Golf Club**, the oldest golf club in the Borders. This 1877 track started as an eleven-hole course, with a complete round being 22 holes. The layout was changed to eighteen holes in 1894, and that's the course that's played today. The 5929-yard course plays on a large hill, but the climbs are gradual; though sometimes the drops are not. Good tee shots are vital for scoring at Hawick, but placement is more important than length. On the 338-yard par 4 fifth hole, *Terrace*, aim your tee shot well right of the left sloping fairway. A "stop board" at the left edge of the light rough kindly (free drop) stops balls from rolling all the way down to the first fairway. The slope is all the defense the hole needs. The views of the Borders hills from the top of the course at the ninth are enthralling. *Pit*, the 292-yard, par 4 sixteenth, is easily drivable because of the hundred-foot drop from tee to a green protected by a bunker left and the pit (a deep grass bunker) right. Tee shot is everything on this hole.

Great golf is a reason to visit the Borders and East Lothian areas, but it is not the only reason.

PUBS

It's easy to find food in the Borders area, and it's not difficult to find interesting places to eat, if you know where to look. In the past five years, Anne and I have found a number of establishments we can recommend for either a lunch or dinner. But first among these is neither the fanciest place nor does it have the best food. What the **Corner House Hotel** in Innerleithen does have is a flavor and friendliness that makes out-of-the-way pubs so inviting. This small village pub was the site of our first evening meal in Scotland the day we arrived in September, 2000. We had just finished a round of golf and were driving through Innerleithen on our way back to the Lindores House, a wonderful B&B in Peebles. Tired, hungry, and excited beyond belief, we saw a sign at the Corner House Hotel saying "Bar Meals Served All Day." That was enough to make us stop. There's nothing fancy about this pub. Ordinary is a more fitting adjective. But "ordinary" is what we were seeking—the real Scottish experience—and boy, did we get it here. We sat down and waited for service. Wrong. After watching other patrons get served after going to the bar, we figured out that if we wanted to eat and drink in Scotland, we'd have to take care of ourselves. A big black labrador retriever lounged underneath an empty bar stool. That we wouldn't see at home. And, while sipping an ale, a young woman worked on what looked like a college term paper or business report while sipping an ale. About the time our food arrived, fish and chip and beef stroganoff (both very savory), we were discovered by a very drunk Scottish lady. Even though inebriated, she was so friendly to ask us about our trip and how we liked what we'd seen of her country so far, that we didn't let her state of intoxication cloud our feelings. After talking with us throughout our meal, she introduced us around to everyone else in the pub, and they in turn started asking us about our trip and America. A quick stop for food had turned into almost two hours of eating and socializing. We forgot how tired we were until back on the road to Peebles. It's a good thing it was still fairly light and only a seven-mile trip. The Corner House Hotel pub may not be fanciest, but we recommend it for its Scottish welcome.

Innerleithen has another worthy pub. In fact, the **Traquair Arms Hotel Pub and Restaurant** has been recognized for its quality fare since the hotel was built as a coaching inn in 1835. Hugh and Marian Anderson, owners of the Traquair Arms since 1984, have maintained that reputation for quality. This rustic, hunting-lodge-style pub and restaurant offers a complete menu in both restaurant and pub, with lots of specials. When we were there last, these included Aberdeen Angus steaks, Beef Wellington, and Chicken stuffed with Stilton (a cheese lovers to-die-for dish). The bar selection is good for both malts and ales, with the specialty of the house being Stuart Ale brewed at the nearby Traquair House Brewery. Food is served from 8:00 in the morning until 9:00 in the evening everyday. The Quair Tea Room serves home baking in the morning and high teas in the afternoons. The Traquair Arms Hotel deserves a visit any time and any day.

Seven miles back in Peebles we've found several pubs that we would return to. One of these, the Keg Lounge/Bar, we offer solely for its view. Right in the heart of the High Street shopping district, this upstairs pub offers a unique view of everyday life in a small town in Scotland. With bar stools and a small bar running along the townside windows, this is a nice place to have a pint or a dram and watch the town below. Anne and I shared fish and chips here one rainy day and watched the bustling activity of noontime. As interesting as the Keg Lounge/Bar is, there are better pubs in Peebles.

Two pubs deserve special mention for their quality and atmosphere. The first is the **Crown Hotel** on High Street at the west end. This family restaurant has four rooms and a bar. The first room has a more open feel and faces the street with windows along the front. The second room is small, intimate and has a fireplace. it's a cozy place for a meal on a cold evening. Room three is a little like a library with walls that are decorated with photos and books. And the fourth room is the sunroom, open and airy. Our choices would be the sunroom for an early meal, or the library room later on. All serve off a fairly extensive pub menu, with several semi-permanent specials. Usually a couple of nightly specials are featured as well. Portions are generous, and we've never been disappointed with the quality. The bar is a good pre- or post-meal spot, usually crowded with locals and dominated by a large-screen TV. We've eaten at the Crown several times, but will always remember the night we dined while a lady and her Scottie terrier (sitting on a chair) dined at the table next to ours.

Another choice in Peebles probably wouldn't let a dog in the dining room, but being that it's Scotland and the dog was a Scottie, you never know. The **Park Hotel Bar**, on Innerleithen Road at the east end of town, is a little more upscale than the Crown. That's not meant to be an indictment of the Crown, just a comment that the Park Hotel offers a different atmosphere. The Park is a more American-style lounge, with plush carpet, stuffed chairs, couches, and something we're beginning to see more of in Scotland, a large nonsmoking section. Food and beverage choices were equal to the atmosphere, which was a little more elegant than normal pub fare. The night we dined they had a special starter on the menu: haggis nest with poached egg served on a cream whisky sauce.

Finally, there is a new eatery in Peebles that we tried in 2004. The **Neidpath Inn**, named after a castle just west of town, has been an estab-

Traquair House near Peebles is the oldest continuously inhabited house in Scotland, and has hosted numerous Scottish kings and queens.

The fifth hole at Peebles Golf Club ends at a green protected by several bunkers.

The downhill fifth hole at Cardrona tempts golfers to try to carry the bunkers in order to shorten the second shot.

Jedburgh Abbey is one of the Border abbeys founded by David I in the 1100s. The massive structure and herb gardens are interesting to tour and the visitor's centre has informative displays.

Melrose Abbey, also founded by David I, is the final resting place for the heart of Robert the Bruce.

The view of Bass Rock is a dominant feature of the fourteenth hole at North Berwick West.

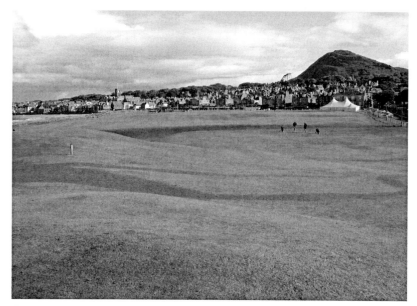

The eighteenth hole at North Berwick West plays back toward the town. The golfers in the fairway are actually playing the first hole on a shared fairway, similar to the first and eighteenth at St. Andrews Old Course.

The tour guide at Robert Smail's Print Shop in Innerleithen, demonstrates the printing process as it would have been done in the 1850s.

lished drinking pub for years. They have finally expanded, featuring two lounge rooms and a patio which overlooks the River Tay for good weather dining. They didn't change the pub much — it's still a dark drinking pub, but the dining areas are bright and modern. The menu was fairly broad, with most of the usual pub food and a few specialties. We ate at Neidpath soon after the dining areas opened and had good meals for good prices, but it was obvious that the food business here was just getting started. One additional attraction which compliments the food is that the inn also hosts musical artists, both traditional and nontraditional, in the new lounge areas. Neidpath Inn will be one to try again.

From Peebles, it's twenty miles to the village of Melrose. This abbey and garden town is a tourist mecca and has several eating and drinking spots. But if you need to take a break from abbey touring, we'd recommend **The Ship Inn,** just off the main town square. This pub chain (there are at least two other Ship Inns, in Broughty Ferry and Stonehaven) offers a safe haven for the tourist. We've been to all three Ship Inns, and they share, the nautical theme and a friendliness toward visitors. The menu in Melrose was a typical pub menu, along with a couple of daily specials on a chalkboard. Most of the patrons were local workers on their noon break. The pub, like the other Ship Inns we've visited, was a lively and friendly place to take a break.

In the other direction from Peebles is the small community of West Linton, with its lovely golf course and a very good public house (pub), worth a stop in its own right. The **Golden Arms Hotel,** at the edge of the village on A702, holds special memories for Anne and I. This is the spot, over a Coke and chips which we shared with two pub dogs, where we first decided to write about our golf and pub experiences. The pub has a hunting-lodge feel, with stone walls, real fireplace, and a mix of furniture. Around the room are library shelves burdened with old books and various antiques. A piano in the corner invites guests to play. The bar serves a high-quality mix of malts and ales, and while the pub menu is pretty typical, you are tempted by several daily specials. We can attest to the fact that the steaks are excellent and the meat pies fresh and delicious. On our last visit, a border collie greeted us, and every time we've been to the Golden Arms conversations have been easy to start. In 2000, we stopped in after golf, and as soon as we stepped in the door, people were asking us if we had found petrol—this was the year of the petrol crisis, when many stations closed down for several days. The Golden Arms is a friendly, homey pub that's worth a visit anytime except when they are closed. between 2:30 and 4:30.

From Peebles toward Edinburgh or Glencorse GC, the A701 passes through Eddleston. There's not much of note here except a fine pub, the **Horseshoe Inn**. Horseshoe is an old coaching-style inn with bar, lounge, and formal dining area. The same limited menu with about six main entrees and a similar number of starters is available in all rooms. What the menu lacks in quantity the kitchen makes up for in quality. We've eaten here a couple of times and been pleased with meals excellently prepared and artistically presented. For those looking for quiet accommodations, the Horseshoe Inn has eight rooms and specializes in trout and salmon-fishing outings.

When in the golf area on the East Lothian coast, don't miss two golf related pubs. First, in Aberlady, on the main road through town (A198), you'll find the **Old Aberlady Inn**. This pub and restaurant has serious association with golfing in the area. An article in an 1893 issue of *Golf* tells the rich history of the Old Aberlady Inn. The inn began as a coaching stop between Edinburgh and North Berwick, and was in the Tait family for more than 80 years. Robert Tait changed the inn into a golfing hotel when the property passed to him from his father. Robert was a founding member of four local golf clubs and was rarely beaten in competition, even though he played with only two clubs. Today the inn honors its golfing heritage with articles, posters, art, and golfing memorabilia. It has several dining areas (pub, conservatory, formal dining room), each with lots of snugs (small booths or semiprivate areas). The menu is extensive—eight pages of entrees, numerous specials, and even wine tasting. We've been pleased with both the lunches and the dinners at Old Aberlady Inn.

A second pub is also on A198, about four miles east in Gullane. Home to the Gullane courses (One, Two, Three, and PeeWee), life in the village is well-chronicled in Curtis Gillespie's *Playing Through: A Year of Life and Links along the Scottish Coast* (Scribner, 2002). Just off the main street and well-signed is the **Old Clubhouse**. Originally a clubhouse for one of the Gullane courses, it is now a golfers' pub, decorated with old photos, golf memorabilia, and golfers telling tales of their latest triumphant or disastrous rounds. With a full bar and a full-range menu (from burgers to steaks), the Old Clubhouse is an inviting spot for a snack or complete meal. Table service is available in the restaurant, but in the pub you have to order at the bar. When we stopped we had a nice lunch and heard about a great victory over an arch rival from the gentleman at the next table.

The Borders area offers great opportunities for golf and eating, and it also provides a wealth of attractions for the tourist.

ATTRACTIONS

The River Tweed winds its way across the Borders country on its way to the sea at Berwick-upon-Tweed in England. This valley is loaded with things to see and do. Dominating the attractions of the area are the Border Abbeys of Melrose, Jedburgh, and Dryburgh. These abbeys alone would be reason enough to visit the region.

Starting at the most southerly of the abbeys, the **Jedburgh Abbey** is just ten miles north of the border with England. The 12th Century Augustinian priory was founded by King David I, and is the best preserved of the Border abbeys. The visitor centre has an educational short video presentation of the history and significance of the abbey. Even on a very rainy day, a tour of the abbey ruins is worth the effort. Driving north seven miles brings the tourist to the remains of **Dryburgh Abbey,** actually visible from St. Boswell Golf Club. This Premonstratensia-, or White Canon-, founded abbey occupies a very beautiful grounds which contrasts the red hues of its stonework with green lawns, white-barked beeches, redwoods, and vivid-colored cedar trees. These ruins, though in a beautiful setting, are much less substantial than the others, but that doesn't diminish their historical significance. Buried in the grounds of the Abbey Church are Sir Walter Scott and Field Marshal Haig (the World War I commander), among others. Traveling north about five miles brings us to the most striking of the Border abbeys, **Melrose Abbey**. It would not be hard to call this abbey, founded by King David I in 1136, the heart of the Border's abbeys. It might be appropriate as well because it is here that the heart of Robert the Bruce, responsible for uniting factions into the real nation of Scotland, is rumored to be buried. In full or muted sunlight, the red stonework at Melrose Abbey takes on different hues. Bright sunshine might be best, but regardless of the weather, there is no bad time to explore Melrose Abbey. Scottish author/poet Sir Walter Scott said about Melrose:

> *When distant Tweed is heard to rave,*
> *And owlet to hoot o'er the dead man's grave,*
> *Then go - but go alone the while -*
> *Then view St. David's ruined pile;*
> *And home returning, soothly swear,*
> *Was ever scene so sad and fair*
> *["Lay of the Last Minstrel"]*

And while wandering the grounds, look for the gargoyle of the pig playing bagpipes on the south side of the nave.

Next to Melrose Abbey is the delightful, walled Priorwood Garden specializing in orchids and flowers for drying (available in the dry flower shop). But for spectacular gardens we suggest a visit to the **Dawyck Botanic Gardens** (pronounced "doe-ick") about eight miles southwest of Peebles (A72 to B712). This 60 acre garden has been part of the Royal Botanic Garden Edinburgh (RBGE) since 1978. The garden has over 300 years of tree plantings, making it one of the world's finest arboreta.

Among Dawyck's most historic plantings are California giant redwoods, Douglas firs, and cedars sent back to Scotland by botanical explorer David Douglas in the early 19th Century. Dawyck has a number of "champion" trees—the stoutest or tallest or oldest of their kind in the UK. There's a pleasant visitors shop and tearoom at the garden as well. You could enjoy an hour or a day visiting Dawyck Gardens.

Heading a different direction out of Peebles, you'll soon encounter two not-to-miss locations. The first, just 3 miles east of Peebles on B7062, is **Kailzie Garden**, a fifteen-acre ground containing tearoom, gift shop, trout pond (with tackle available for rent), and a walled garden. It is the walled garden which rightly attracts the most attention. Though not as large as Dawyck, Kailzie Garden makes up for it in variety of flora. Be sure to take time to look at the spectacular tropical and semitropical plants housed in the large greenhouses. This garden, tucked away on a small back road, is the stereotypical *Alice-in-Wonderland*-type walled garden.

Back on the B7062, it's just four miles to **Traquair House**. One of the Great Houses of Scotland, Traquair is acknowledged to be the oldest continuously inhabited house in Scotland, tracing its heritage back to 1100 when it was built as a hunting lodge. Traquair Castle, as it was originally known, has played host to as many as 15 Scottish Kings or Queens including the tragic Mary Queen of Scots. Currently, Catherine Connstable Maxwell Stuart is the twenty-first in the Stuart line to oversee Traquair. Traquair (from *tra* meaning a "dwelling" or "hamlet"; and from the *Quair*, a tributary of the River Tweed, which runs near the back of the house) is now both a museum and guesthouse. Traquair's museum grounds contain a crafts workshop, a cottage tearoom (built in 1745), picnic area, maze, wooded walk, operating brewery, and the house itself. Several interesting rooms are open to visitors to the main house. There is a Priest's Room, where the family could secretly practice Catholicism, and which has a secret panel that reveals a hidden staircase, which allowed the priest to escape. The library was particularly fascinating. Created between 1700 and 1740, the library houses over 3000 volumes. The cataloguing system is unique: portraits of philosophers and writers indicate the various sections, and all the books in each section are labeled and numbered under the portrait. For instance, all the books under the philosopher Aristotle are labeled with ARIS, then a number indicating the shelf, and a second number indicating the book's position on that shelf. ARIS 8-20 would be a book under Aristotle's portrait, eight shelves down, 20 books over. Ingenious! As a guesthouse, Traquair has three rooms that are let as a B&B. Our first year in Scotland, Anne and I had booked a night at Traquair without knowing too much about it except that it was a special place. At the ticket kiosk, we told the lady attendant that we were booked in for the night, and she said, "Oh, you're the guests. Drive on up to the gate." At the gate we were greeted by a younger lady who said that she was the house attendant, adding, "You must the guests." That was the second time we had heard the singular "the guests." We asked and were told that only one room had been rented that night, and we would have the House to ourselves (except for the attendant and the Stuarts who live in a different wing). This is an exceptional experience! To live like royalty, even for just one night, was fantastic. Our bedroom was adorned and furnished by nothing younger than 200 years old (except the TV and toilet facilities). The bed was a lovely, huge, canopied four-poster. We also had use of our own sitting room filled with antiques and Stuart-family history. In the morning, breakfast was served for just the two of us in the Still Room, decorated with fine porcelain in hutches in each corner. Lovely! Traquair House is a must-see and must-do. It would be well worth the price, but book early because few rooms are available.

Now we go from one Great House to the next. Fourteen miles east of Traquair House is **Abbotsford**, the wonderful stone fantasy of author Sir Walter Scott. Built in 1812, the "Conundrum Castle ... this romance of a house," as Scott called it, was his dream castle. Bristling with turrets and baronial gables, Abbotsford is a dream to visit. The rooms open to the public are stuffed with historic antiquities. In one glass case I saw Napoleon's pen case, a lock of Admiral Nelson's hair, and a comb lost on the Culloden battlefields. One of the best opportunities during the tour of Abbotsford is that photography is allowed. In almost all other castles, a NO PHOTO rule applies. Being allowed to photograph rooms like the beautiful library was a real joy. Outside, a splendid garden and enticing tearoom add to the experience.

One of the most impressive historic sites in Scotland is not far from Glencorse Golf Club in Penicuik. **Rosslyn Chapel** in Roslin was built in 1446 and has been described as a "Tapestry in Stone." Thousands of some of the most impressive stone carvings in Scotland, if not Europe, adorn practically every inch of the chapel walls, ceilings, and pillars. Numerous myths and legends surround Rosslyn Chapel. It has been linked to the Knights Templar, who guarded pilgrims on their journeys to the Holy Land, as well as to the beginnings of the Masonic movement, and is rumored to be the burial place for the Holy Grail. It is also said that the chapel is haunted by both a Black Knight on horseback and a Lady in White. Whether you see the ghosts or find the Holy Grail or not, Rosslyn Chapel is one of the most memorable sites in all Europe.

Again I've saved the most unique attraction for last. To be worth our time doesn't mean something must be as ancient as Traquair or as spectacular as Melrose Abbey. Small can be worthy as well. In this case **Robert Smail's Printing Works** in Innerleithen is one of best attractions we've seen in Scotland. This print shop was started in 1866 by Robert Smail to take care of the printing needs of the Peebles-Innerleithen-Walkerburn area. The print shop was turned over to the National Trust for Scotland in 1986. Now the shop is open for tours of the office, the composing room, and the machine room. The office is where the day-to-day clerical work of the business was conducted. Now, though, it is a museum of the community because Smail kept a copy of every single item he printed—wedding invitations, advertisements, public notices. We also saw a register for the Titanic listing all the people in the area who booked passage on that fateful voyage. In the composing room we met a young lady who had recently graduated from Edinburgh University in graphic design and was working in the print shop, half as tour guide and half as composer. The shop is still working on special printing jobs. She was a wonderfully witty, knowledgeable, and enthusiastic guide. To demonstrate the process, she had volunteers set some type and print their work. In the composing room we learned trivia, like where the terms "upper-" and "lower- case" letters originated: from their position in storage trays, capitals in the "upper" boxes, and small letters in the "lower." Then on to the machine room where we saw operating presses from as early as 1880. The tour of Robert Smail's Print Shop in Innerleithen is certainly an hour and a half well spent.

From the Abbeys to Abbotsford, from Traquair to Dawyck, the Borders abounds in beauty and history.

GOLF COURSE INFORMATION

Course:	**Innerleithen Golf Club**
Style & Length:	Moorland, 3033 yds, par 35
Price:	20GBP/day
Availability:	Just show up
Phone:	(01896) 830951

Course:	**Peebles Golf Club**
Style & Length:	Parkland, 6160 yds, par 70
Price:	20GBP
Availability:	Visitors welcome, but not on Saturday
Phone:	(01721) 720197
Web:	www.peeblesgolfclub.co.uk

Course:	**West Linton Golf Club**
Style & Length:	Moorland, 6132 yds, par 69
Price:	25GBP

Availability:	Weekdays anytime, PM weekends
Phone:	(01968) 660256
Web:	www.wlgc.co.uk

Course:	**St. Boswell Golf Club**
Style & Length:	Parkland, 2625 yds, par 34
Price:	18GBP/day
Availability:	Easy to get on, no trolleys
Phone:	(01835) 823527
Web:	www.scot-borders.co.uk

Course:	**Cardrona Golf Club**
Style & Length:	Inland, 6856 yds, par 68
Price:	20GBP
Availability:	Book ahead to be sure
Phone:	(01896) 833715

Course:	**Glencorse Golf Club**
Style & Length:	Inland hilly, 5217 yds, par 64
Price:	19GBP
Availability:	Call ahead
Phone:	(01968) 677177

Course:	**Kilspindie Golf Club**
Style & Length:	Links, 5480 yds, par 66
Price:	29GBP
Availability:	Busy, call ahead
Phone:	(01875) 870358

Course:	**North Berwick West Golf Club**
Style & Length:	Links, 6420 yds, par 71
Price:	42GBP
Availability:	Book ahead
Phone:	(01620) 892135
Web:	www.northberwickgolfclub.com

Course:	**Hawick Golf Club**
Style & Length:	Inland hilly, 5929 yds, par 68
Price:	20GBP
Availability:	Fairly easy to get on
Phone:	(01450) 372293
Web:	www.scot-borders.co.uk

Chapter Eight:
Southern Scotland
along the Solway Firth

Golf: Powfoot, Southerness, Silloth on Solway, Wigtown & Bladnoch, St. Medan, Girvan

Pubs: Powfoot Golf Hotel, Huntingdon Hotel, The Royal Hotel, Bladnoch Inn, Hope and Anchor, King's Arms, Highland Laddie

Attractions (for when you can't golf): Caelaverock Castle, Dumfries, Sweetheart Abbey, Kirkcudbright, Threave Castle, Cardoness Castle, Cairn Holy, Castle Kennedy Gardens

GOLF

Visitors to Scotland seek out the Highlands with their lonely, haunted glens, whisky and castle trails. They head to the islands filled with history and myth. Also they relish the Borders, Lothians, and Fife especially for the golf. But one region often neglected is rich with historical sights and filled with wonderful golfing adventures for those willing to explore. This is southern Scotland, especially the Dumfries and Galloway area along the shores of the Solway Firth.

This area is filled with wonderful links and seaside golf courses that are as good as the famous links of the Fife and Moray Firth, but not nearly as crowded. In September, we've dropped in and played even the most famous of the Solway courses without pre-booking.

Beginning our tour of the Solway Firth courses nearest the main north-south thoroughfare, variously labeled M74 (near Glasgow) and

A74M (in the south), we stop at **Powfoot Golf Club,** near Annan in Dumfriesshire. "The Powfoot Links are a fine natural course with springy turf and excellent greens." This 1922 Powfoot Golf Club guide description could have been written yesterday. Powfoot, off B724 about 3 miles west of Annan (on A75 between Gretna and Dumfries), is a predominately links course, with most holes offering views of the Solway Firth and the English Cumbrian Fells (or mountains). An early James Braid design (1903 for the original nine holes), it plays back and forth across the linksland rather than out and back, with fairly open fairways, strategic bunkering, and the ever-present wind which always seems against your shot. The third hole, *Shore*, is a 265-yard par 3 which often plays into the prevailing wind—a daunting hole which most of us mortals would play as a two-shotter. The ninth hole, a 402-yard par 4 named *Crater*, has as a hazard a huge German bomb crater short of the green. This isn't the only remnant of World War II on the course. The last four holes are relatively flat and more parkland in design as a result of use as Victory Gardens during the war. *Sahara*, the 313-yard par 4 eleventh, begins with a blind tee shot, with ample of bailout room to the right, the direction the wind will push your ball. Climb the tee platform to check for golfers in the landing area before you tee off. The green is protected by hummocks as well as a large bunker. One player commented after a round at Powfoot that the course "is a hidden delight for any golfer seeking an enjoyable day's golf and an easy test on the legs." When you finish your round visit the comfortable clubhouse or browse the well-stocked pro shop. If you want to stay in the area, check out the nearby Powfoot Golf Hotel which has golfer specials and hearty evening meals.

From Annan it's fifteen miles (on A75) to Dumfries, and then a further 16 miles (on A710) to the best-known of Scotland's southern courses. **Southerness Golf Club** is reported to be the first championship-caliber course built in Britain after World War II. The course was opened in 1947 and has been gaining in stature ever since. Famous golf architect Mackenzie Ross created Southerness to be fair but challenging. Many players rank this as one of the most difficult tests in Scotland. When we played, on a cloudy day with only light wind, I thought the course was very playable (don't read that as easy) for a mid-handicap player. The views of the firth and the Cumbrian mountains alone would be worth the trip, but it is really the golf that people should come for. Bunkers (lots of bunkers, all in play), heather and gorse, and the weather add to the difficulties found on the interesting links holes at Southerness. Several holes here deserve special note. The 371-yard, par 4 eighth has one of the best guarded-greens I've encountered. Five bunkers near or around the green provide trouble, and mounding around the green adds to the challenge. A precise shot is needed to thread your way safely onto the green. Another fun hole is the twelfth, a 421-yard par 4. On this dogleg right the tee shot must find its way past two bunkers on the right and one on the left. Bunkers right protect the green on this long two-shotter. The par threes at Southerness are outstanding as well. For example, the fifteenth at 217 yards, plays into the prevailing wind, and a fore bunker and five surrounding bunkers make the green a difficult target to reach. With eight par 4s longer than 400 yards, it's easy to understand why Southerness GC is consistently rated in the top twenty in Scotland.

Before continuing west I suggest a hop across the Solway Firth. Actually, a drive back around the firth via Carlisle, England, is a more practical way to visit Silloth on Solway and its exceptional links course. As value for your money, this 1892 course is hard to beat. **Silloth on Solway Golf Club** is a members-only club which allows visitors who are members of other clubs. It is a true links course, with four holes set along the firth, which is visible from all holes. At 6634 yards, this par-72 course is not overly long, but plenty of heather and gorse, along with generous fairways and a few tough bunkers, make it a real challenge.

At Silloth, the par four, 371-yard third hole, named *Criffel* after the 1868-feet peak across the firth near Southerness GC, is characteristic of the par fours on the course. A blind tee shot between two sand hills starts the hole. The second shot is to a plateau green. No bunkers protect the hole, but plenty of gorse does if you stray off line. The ninth hole, a 144-yard par 3, seems an easy hole, except that the tee shot needs to avoid the seven bunkers in play. A dramatic hole is number thirteen, a par 5 of 511 yards. The first shot is a long carry over gorse to a generous fairway. From here the hole tightens as you get closer to the small elevated green. This hole is followed by another par five, and both play into the wind. Silloth on Solway GC isn't in Scotland, but it is Scottish in design and friendliness. Besides, it's definitely out-of-the-way and worth the effort to get find. Host of two British Ladies'Amateurs, it prompted one player to exclaim, "It's the best links course I've played in the UK, including four of the Open venues!"

Back across the Solway Firth and again heading west from Dumfries, we come to Wigtown, a nice town for a bookish visit and a quick round of golf. At the west end is the **Wigtown and Bladnoch Golf Club**. This 2731-yard, par-34, nine-hole track plays on a hill with holes three and five playing uphill and four and six playing dramatically down. There are a few bunkers; otherwise, the hills, trees, and small greens present the challenges here. One of the best holes at Wigtown is the 275-yard par 4 fourth. The wide landing area of the downhill tee shot is protected by large trees on each side. Strong, prevailing winds make the hole longer than its downhill yardage would indicate. The other downhill hole, number six, a 362-yard par 4, is a sharp dogleg left. The test off the tee is to avoid the trees on the inner corner of the dog-leg, while still taking enough club to get past those trees, but not so much that you run out of fairway. It's an interesting shot which, depending upon the wind, could be very different. When at the top of the course on the tee box of six, be sure to look north to spot the Wigtown Martyr's Monument, which is an eloquent remembrance of two Covenanter women who, in 1685, were left to drown at the stake in the estuary flats. Wigtown and Bladnoch GC is not a course to go out of your way for, but if you are in the area, it is worth a round—just drop your money in the honesty box and have a go.

Sixteen miles south and west along the A746-A747 from Wigtown is a hidden gem of a golf course. Near the village of Monreith, **St. Medan Golf Club** is a seaside clifftop course, similar to Anstruther on the Fife. The course plays along Monreith Bay with great views of Luce Bay and the Irish Sea. At 2277 yards and a par of 32, it's typical of Scotland's short, challenging golf courses. A few bunkers, five blind shots (more if you are off line), and separate tee boxes for those who can play eighteen holes, characterize the course. All the holes at St. Medan are well-designed with wonderful views, but several stand out. First, number four, a 274-yard par 4, called *Well* after the old well behind the green, is a spectacular risk/reward hole. The green is reach-able, even with a fairway metal (The wind usually helps and the hole plays downhill.), but there is trouble all around. I like the hole because I hit the green two-for-two in my round. The seventh, *Lagg*, is a 273-yard par 4 where the initial shot needs to lay-up at the bottom of a knock between the tee and the green. Big hitters might be tempted to go for the green. Don't! The rough on the knock is unforgiving, and the green is a hard target to find, even on the second shot when using the aiming pole. The last hole finishes the round nicely. *Hame* is a down-hill (take one less club), 186-yard par 3, with a fairly large green pro-tected by five bunkers in front and on both sides. St. Medan GC is an honesty-box course with a small clubhouse and a few trolleys to hire. It is definitely a course to go out of your way for. Beautiful scenery and interesting golf holes make St. Medan a worthy excursion.

The last course for this section is not along the Solway Firth. Instead, **Girvan Municipal Golf Club** sits along the North Channel between Scotland and Ireland. As golfers explore the Ayrshire coast, the courses of Royal Troon, Turnberry, and Prestwick get most of the atten-tion. Five miles south of Turnberry, though, is an interesting, inexpen-sive combination links-and-parkland course which deserves more notice. At Girvan GC the starter's shack is next to the public beach and the first hole, while the modern clubhouse is up the hill above the eighth green. The first eight holes are narrow links holes, and nine to eighteen play as wide parkland holes. The links holes tend to be more interesting, but the parkland ten are fun as well, with at least one being unique. The fifth hole is a 171-yard par 3 named *Ailsa Craig* for the famous rock off shore. Turnberry is known for its views of the Ailsa Craig, when actually, Girvan's views are even better. The tee shot at the fifth is straight out toward the famous rock to a green protected by three bunkers. The next hole, a 299-yard par 4, plays along the edge of the beach for its entire length. Not a favorite hole with slicers. Number eight, the last of the links holes, called *Right Scunner*, is a long par 3 with a large, grass-covered dune on the left and a green protected by a deep bunker.

Leaving the eighth green you must walk past the clubhouse to the start of the parkland holes at number nine. These are very playable holes, but the most interesting is the eighteenth, *Ower at Last*, a par 3 of only 137 yards. The name could mean simply that the round is now over or it could be your comment when you get your ball in play. From an elevated tee, a first shot needs to get up quickly to clear the large trees that rise up in front of the tee box. If that shot isn't difficult enough, the green which can barely be seen through the trees, has a deep bunker on the right. Girvan Municipal GC is a worthwhile stop for a round. Even though the course gets lots of play from locals, we had no trouble getting a game at midday on a Sunday.

Whether it's a village course like Wigtown, a muni like Girvan, the hidden gem of St. Medan, the championship links of Southerness, or one of the many other interesting courses in the area, plan to play some great golf in Scotland's southern areas.

PUBS

Besides being rich in good golf, the southern Scotland region is also rich in pleasant pubs, starting at Powfoot with the **Powfoot Golf Hotel**. Located adjacent to the links course, the Powfoot Golf Hotel makes a good stop after a round. Originally a Victorian villa, the hotel has 16 rooms and offers dining in three different settings. The Conservatory, the Bistro, and the Bunker Bar all offer the same complete menu which includes cajun, curries, and Scottish dishes. The Venison Haggis looked interesting, though I didn't try it. Be sure to check the chalk board for numerous daily specials.

In Dumfries, many pleasing eateries can be enjoyed in the downtown area. There is also good dining in the guesthouse hotels which are just out of main shopping district. We found a fine meal at the **Huntingdon Hotel** on St. Mary's Road, about three blocks from downtown. The bright modern, lounge was typical of small hotel guesthouses, as is the complete menu. What distinguishes Huntingdon Hotel lounge from others is its waitress. She served guests in the bar section, the lounge, and the dining room. She had a smile for everyone and was quick with a joke or a story. Food here is high quality—one of the best lentil soups I've had. Whether you stay in the small hotels or not, many like Huntingdon Hotel are good bets for pub meals.

Sticking with the hotel theme, the next stop we'd suggest is **The Royal Hotel** on Main Street in Kirkcudbright (kirk-coo-brie). A main artist and tourist center, Kirkcudbright is on the main southern tourist/golfer route. The Victorian pub lounge and dining room at the Royal Hotel serve different menus. Whereas the dining room is formal, the pub is comfortable with overstuffed chairs and couches, small tables, and an excellent lounge menu. The pub is a great stop between golf rounds or as a break from sightseeing.

When Anne and I are visiting a new locale, we generally like to try a different place for each meal. Many times, though, we find a spot so good that we just have to go back. Such a pub is the **Bladnoch Inn**, a mile from Wigtown, directly across from Bladnoch Distillery. This is a locals' pub in the sportsman-lodge style. The walls were covered with fishing art and wildlife plates. Make your meal selection from the full menu and order in the bar. You'll be called to the dining room when your food is ready. One night we split a very tasty seafood platter which included cockles, mussels, crab, smoked and baked salmon, peppered mackerel, and halibut. Well prepared and reasonably priced.

Across the Solway Firth near Silloth on Solway GC, Anne and I had the good fortune to find a trio of small village pubs within about five miles of each other. All three served excellent meals in quaint, rustic settings. **The Porthole Restaurant and Hope and Anchor Pub** in Port of Carlisle, the **King's Arm** in Bowness-on-Solway, and the **Highland Laddie** in Glassen each sits in the heart of its village. On recommendation of our B&B host, we tried all three and were never disappointed. So close are these pubs that one night when one was having a cooking problem, the manager called the neighboring village and booked us a dinner spot in its pub. As an example of the three, I'll highlight the Highland Laddie. It features three seating areas, fireplace, is decorated with local paintings, and filled with a mix of locals and travelers. The bar is standing-room only, and in one of the back rooms a local card club often plays at three of the tables. Everyone is talking to everyone else. We visited with a South African engineer from Kent, who just happen to have a daughter working in the States about 20 miles from our home. When he left, we visited about golf with a local couple who sat down at the table next to us. The food at all three pubs was well-prepared. These three pubs may have been in England, but they were Scottish in feel and friendliness.

ATTRACTIONS

The swing west on A75 from the main north-south freeway (M74) begins at Gretna Green, famous as a Scottish wedding centre, particularly for young English couples. While Gretna Green is a tourist trap, the more adventuresome tourists will head west to **Caelaverock Castle** (*Lark's Nest*), about nine miles southeast of Dumfries (signposted from A75). The substantial ruins of this 13th Century Maxwell family castle have a complete moat around them. The grounds of the castle also host a locally run tearoom known for its homemade bakery goods.

From Caerlaverock it's a short drive to **Dumfries**, the largest of southern Scotland's towns with a population just over 31,000. Interesting sites abound in Dumfries, mostly concerning poet Robert Burns, who died here in 1796. The Burns statue dominates the north end of High Street and the Burns Center is just across the Nith River. West from Dumfries on the A710 (the coastal route which follows the Solway Firth), **Sweetheart Abbey** in New Abbey is only an eight-mile drive. This 13th Century Cistercian abbey gets its name from foundress Dervorgilla, who had the abbey built in remembrance of her husband, John Balliol—hence the name Sweetheart. The ruin is spectacular, with great striding arches, semicircular arches, and the stout tower. Just down the road from the abbey is the New Abbey Cornmill, an interesting place to learn about early production of that Scottish staple, oatmeal.

Still on the coastal route (now A711), **Kirkcudbright** is a village in which to tarry. This artist village set on the banks of the Dee River (one of five in Scotland) is a major tourist destination. Besides the historic MacLellan's Castle in the heart of the village, the main attraction is the art shops. The 17th Century Tollbooth has been transformed into a serious art center, with audiovisual show, artist studios, and extensive displays of local artists' works. After shopping in Kirkcudbright head toward Castle Douglas.

Two miles south of Castle Douglas on B736 is the parking area for **Threave Castle**. The three-quarter-mile walk is well-rewarded by the impressive ruins of the 14th Century former residence of the Black Douglases. Ring the bell at the small dock and the Historic Scotland steward will cross the River Dee in a small boat to ferry you over to the

The statue of poet Robbie Burns dominates the town square in Dumfries.

Sahara is a 313-yard par 4, which is typical of the links holes at Powfoot Golf Club.

There is no lake on the 200-yard par 3 fifteenth hole at Powfoot; though, two ball-gobbling bunkers lurk right of the green.

Cairn Holy Chambered Cairns, west of Cardoness Castle, is a Neolithic burial monument with a commanding view over the Solway Firth.

Castle Kennedy Gardens, near Stranraer, which have been described as "Too form'd for Nature--too wild for Art," is a bountiful display of rhoddies in the spring.

Silloth on Solway may be across the firth in England, but holes like the 371-yard third, are very much Scottish in style.

St. Medans Golf Club was a pleasant surprise, and the green at the eighth hole shows some of the features of the course.

Caerlaverock Castle, with its moat, stands in a pleasant, parkland setting by the north shore of the Solway Firth.

island site of the castle. The castle is interesting, photogenic, and spectacular. Definitely, worth going out of the way for.

Two interesting sites to visit as you continue along the coastal route (now the A75) are **Cardoness Castle** and **Cairn Holy**. The castle, built in the mid-1400s, is prominently set on a rock outcrop overlooking the tidal marshes of Fleet Bay. Cairn Holy, six miles further west, consists of two preserved, chambered burial cairns. The elevation of these Neolithic monuments affords wonderful views of the surrounding hills and the Solway Firth. The day Anne and I visited the cairns, an RAF fighter on a low-level training flight seemed to be actually below our position as he flew by. Breathtaking!

A fine place to set up a base to explore the western end of the firth is **Wigtown** (on coastal route A714). In the early 1990s, when the distillery and other industries closed, the town was in danger of dying. It was decided to turn Wigtown into Scotland's Booktown (modeled after Hay-on-Wye, a village in Wales). The scheme to encourage booksellers and publishers to locate here has led to a rousing September book festival, hosted by the more than 20 book-related companies now located in this small community. For book lovers this is a dangerous place! Anne and I limited ourselves to a couple of books each. It was a limit which we rapidly exceeded. While you are in the area, try to find time to visit Scotland's most southerly distillery, the recently reopened Bladnoch Distillery, only a mile from town.

Back on A75 is **Castle Kennedy Gardens**, three miles east of the ferry town of Stranraer. With the ruins of both the castle home of the Kennedy clan and those of the 19th Century baronial Lochinch Castle on the grounds, this more-than-200-acre site offers gardens, lochans, sweeping lawns, and tree-lined avenues for visitors. In the spring, the 1842-restored garden is a magnificent display of tree-sized rhododendrons. It's easy to spend a couple of hours wandering the the grounds, yet still know that you haven't seen everything.

From great links and seaside golf, to pubs with great food and local atmosphere, to wondrous castles and gardens, the area along the Solway Firth in southern Scotland is well worth planning to visit.

GOLF COURSE INFORMATION

Course: **Powfoot Golf Club**
Style and Length: Links/Parkland, 6255 yds, par 71
Price: 23GBP
Availability: Accepts visitors, call ahead
Phone: (01461) 700276

Course: **Southerness Golf Club**
Style and Length: Links, 6566 yds, par 69
Price: 32GBP
Availability: Call ahead
Phone: (01387) 880677

Course: **Silloth on Solway Golf Club**
Style and Length: Links, 6618 yds, par 72
Price: 25GBP
Availability: Accepts visitors who are members of another club
Phone: (01697) 331304

Course: **Wigtown & Bladnoch Golf Club**
Style and Length: Parkland, 2731 yds, par 34
Price: 15GBP for 18
Availability: Honesty box
Phone: (01988) 403354

Course: **St. Medan Golf Club**
Style and Length: Seaside, 2277 yds, par 32
Price: 15GBP all day
Availability: Honesty box
Phone: (01988) 700358

Course: **Girvan Municipal Golf Club**
Style and Length: Links/Parkland, 5064 yds, par 64
Price: 13GBP
Availability: Easy to get on
Phone: (01465) 714346
Web Site: www.golfsouthayrshire.com/girvan.html

Chapter Nine:
Ayr, Isle Arran, and Kintyre

GOLF: Belleisle, Seafield, Maybole Municipal, Doon Valley, Corrie, Lamlash, Whiting Bay, Shiskine, Macrie Bay, Carradale, Macrihanish, Dalmally

PUBS: Brig o' Doon House Hotel, Wildings Hotel, Brodick Bar, Piershead Tavern, Lagg Inn, The Pantry, Catacol Hotel Pub, MacGrochan's Bar, Coasters, Oban Inn, Suie Lodge

ATTRACTIONS (for when you can't golf): Culzean Castle, Crossraguel Abbey, Burns Country, Arran Shopping, Brodick Castle, Stones, Arduaine Gardens, Dunstaffnage Castle, Oban/Mull/Iona

GOLF

Forty minutes south from Glasgow International Airport is Ayrshire, a region steeped in the history of Scotland and the history of golf. It's here the tourist will find magnificent castles and abbeys. It's here, too, one can trace the footsteps of the great Scottish poet Robert Burns. And it is here where the golfer can find the Open Championship courses of Turnberry and Royal Troon, and the historic Prestwick. From Ayrshire as well one can jump off the mainland to explore Scotland in miniature, the Isle of Arran.

Let's begin our out-of-the-way tour in the main town of the region, Ayr. We find a real gem of Scottish golf here. **Belleisle Golf Club** is well recognized by some, but unknown to many. This course has been called the best parkland public course in Scotland. It's good enough to host a yearly Scottish PGA tournament and has hosted the prestigious Senior Scottish PGA Championship. The reason it remains relatively unknown is that it is overshadowed by the links golf in the area at Royal Troon, Turnberry, and Prestwick. The visitor looking for good golf should not overlook Belleisle (bell-isle). Designed in 1927 by James Braid, the course starts at the impressive Belleisle Hotel, where the large pro shop and starter's office resides on the lower floor. The course plays out through fairways lined with huge beech trees, with the Curtecan Burn cutting across and alongside several holes. The course is also well-bunkered, making it a worthwhile challenge. Don't be fooled, it looks easier than it plays. The start may seem daunting, but really can get the round off to a strong beginning. The 471-yard, par 5 first hole is relatively easy, and it is followed by a second par 5 at 470 yards, made more difficult by very strategic bunkering. The sixth, *The Lang Drop*, a 429-yard par 4, offers the best views of the Firth of Clyde and Isle Arran, and is also rated the most difficult. Even though downhill from the tee, the fairway is guarded by bunkers located right in the landing area, and the green is protected by bunkers front and back. *Summerfield*, the 431-yard, par 4 thirteenth is another challenging hole. The tee shot plays uphill, but the green is hidden from the second shot, and again it's protected by good bunkering. Belleisle is a wonderful example of Braid's work—challenging, inexpensive, yet fun play. It's well worth the stop.

Easier to get on is Belleisle's sister course, **Seafield Golf Club,** which shares the pro shop. The course opened in 1904 as a nine-hole course designed by James Braid. Those holes are now six through thirteen. It was later expanded, again by Braid. The first five holes play as parkland, the next eight as links, and the last five again as parkland. It's a classic Braid design, with challenging short par fours. Several of the locals we talked to actually like this course better than the more known Belleisle. I liked them both. I found the sixth, *Roon the Wa'*, to be more intimidating than difficult. This 297-yard par 4 sweeps right in an arc with a wall (*Wa'*) along its entire length (OB). Mounds and heavy rough make finding the fairway important. Holes fourteen and sixteen are the kind that make Braid's courses interesting. *Doon 'N Roon* is a 259-yard par 4 on which a large fir hangs out into the driving area, making the tee shot more difficult. The green is drivable with a fairway metal, but the tree left and bunker right of the green add to the adventure. Sixteen, *Braid's Plateau*, a par 4 at 265 yards, plays down from a slightly elevated tee to a burn (should not be in play), then steeply up to the green, protected by three bunkers only one of which is visible from seventy yards out. Classic Braid design, with a tree in the direct line to avoid the slope to the right. The pair of courses in Ayr, Belleisle and Seafield, would make a great day of golf; then plan to stop at the Tam O' Shanter Pub next to the pro shop.

Nine miles south from Ayr on A77 is the village of Maybole. Not much to distinguish this village, the same can't be said of the golf course there. Certainly not in the same league with Belleisle or Seafield, the 9-hole **Maybole Municipal Golf Club,** nevertheless, is enjoyable to play. Cut into a small tract of land, Maybole has some of the narrowest fairways—some of them a mere 20 yards wide their entire length! The trouble off the fairway is thick grass that likes to hide balls and grab clubs. In fact, one of the charms of this course was tromping through the rough between parallel holes, helping golfers from the other hole find their balls, as they help you. On one hole we were looking for one player's Top Flite with no success. As I came down this same hole, I found his ball and, two holes later, returned it to him. By that time we felt like old friends. He did say the rough was higher than normal that year because of heavy rains. Particularly interesting was the fifth hole, a 340-yard par 4 called *Monument.* A parish monument to World War I victims sits at the edge of the hole. The tee shot is uphill to a narrow fairway, with a blind second shot over a burn to the green, protected by a grass bunker. Aim about ten yards right of the monument for the second shot. Number eight is a challenging short hole. (The type I'd like to see more of in the States.) It's a 275-yard par 4 dogleg right where the tee shot faces a cross bunker about 200 yards out. The green is tucked behind a stand of trees on the right side. An effective tee shot would be over the left side of the bunker, neither too far left nor too long. A great short hole with lots of ways to find trouble. A commuter train line runs right beside the course and offers an interesting diversion. Maybole Golf Club is quite a find at 6GBP for nine holes (and they didn't charge for a trolley). Golf at Maybole is fun and uncomplicated, with interesting views of the surrounding area.

Another village golf course in the area and worth a mention is **Doon Valley Golf Course** in Patna, about eight miles southeast of Ayr. Founded in 1937, the inland Doon Valley course is a 2928-yard par 35, with numerous holes which cross other holes. The fifth hole, a 135-yard par 3, is a most unusual design. A large ditch or canyon runs diagonally the length of the hole, with a large tree about halfway on the right. The result is that the hole is almost all carry to a small green protected by one bunker. Over the green is a steep drop off and to the right is OB. Ladies play a tee at the right of the hole, which avoids the canyon but plays 177 yards. For a couple, it's like each playing a very different hole. The course has no trolleys for hire, but they let Anne borrow a member's trolley. No bunker rakes were available either—smooth out the bunkers the best you can, and try to stay out of others. We did get a cute reaction from two locals coming off the course as we were starting play. One said to the other, "They're Americans and they've come to play our course!"

From Ayrshire it's an easy ride aboard a Caledonian MacBrayne ferry over to the Isle of Arran. The ferry terminal at Ardrossan is your departure point for the 45-minute ride over to Brodick on the island. Arran is called "Scotland in Miniature" because you find a representative bit of everything there: lowlands, highlands, linksland. As for golf, the same is true. Arran has a little bit of every type of golf. For a small island, whose perimeter road is about 60 miles around, Arran is rich in golf. Coming over on the ferry last year, we saw many people on foot with their golf clubs, probably intending to play Brodick Golf Club, about half a mile from the ferry terminal. The island has seven courses: three eighteen-hole, three nine-hole courses, and one other. All of the courses on Arran are worth playing, but some are more worthy.

After arriving in Brodick,—the only community of any size on the island, and which has the only ATM (good thing the island is not too big),—drive north on the only main road, A841, for about eight miles, through the coastal community of Corrie, to the next village, Sannox. The clerk at the cheese factory directed us to the course, and said, "Around every corner is a different, but lovely view." Near Sannox you'll find the **Corrie Golf Club** (small sign and a sharp turn into the course). Corrie Golf Club, built in 1892, is a nine-hole course set below Goatfell Peak. The course is surrounded on three sides by mountains and faces the Sound of Bute on the fourth. This course is typical of small community courses built in this time period. It follows the contour of the land, and holes cross over other holes. Pay at the tearoom if it's open, or leave your money in the honesty box and play away. Before you tee off on number one, study the course map posted on the approach to the tee box. Number two, a 135-yard par 3, is the most unusual hole. The tee shot must cross over the first fairway to a green hidden behind a large tree and to the side of the elevated third tee. Except by the luckiest of shots, you can't reach the green on your first shot because of the tree. I imagine that when the course was built, the green would have been in sight, with only a small tree to contend with. But small trees grow into big trees. I also would believe that locals know the tricks of where to hit, but for me it was a 135-yard two-shotter. Par was still there for the taking if I'd made the putt. The course climbs gently uphill for the first five holes, level for the sixth, and downhill from seven. The sixth is a good example of what is called a "gun platform green"—a green cut into the hillside. Besides the quaintness of an old Scottish course, the mountain scenery of ferns and heather and peaks is spectacular.

Back through Brodick, the hilltop **Lamlash Golf Club** is four miles further south. The two-story clubhouse looks over the first tee and the eighteenth green with a small pro shop downstairs and pub upstairs. The course is hilly and buggies are available, but it's not too difficult a walk (only a little huff and puff). Designed by St. Andrew's Willie Auchterlonie in 1896, the course was redesigned by Willie Fernie which makes Lamlash a course of good pedigree and Arran's oldest eighteen-hole course. Lamlash's wonderful vistas of the village and the Holy Island off Arran's coast prompted one player to say, "The view must be one of the best in golf!" The course features some tough par threes, including the tenth, a 215-yard dogleg leg which makes it impossible to see the green from the tee; and the the fifteenth, a 233-yard hole with a blind tee shot over an old rock quarry and then downhill to the green. You'll notice the uphill holes, but it's the downhill shots which are dramatic. Especially exciting is the ninth, *Mullaig Mhor*, a 270-yard par 4, where the green can be seen from the tee, but the landing area can't.

A little further south is **Whiting Bay Golf Club**. To reach the course, turn left at the sign in the village of Whiting Bay and go up the small road forever. It seems like forever, although it's really only 3/4 of a mile. Whiting Bay Golf Club is really golf on the top of a mountain. It reminded us of Roundwood G. C. on Roundwood Mountain, County Wicklow, Ireland, another top-of-the-mountain course. With climbs a little steeper than Lamlash, this is a course where you might be advised to take a powered buggy—after all, you are on vacation. This inland (parkland and moorland) eighteen-hole course has stunning views of Ayrshire (Almost directly across the Firth of Clyde is Prestwick.) and the Holy Island, as well as town and the shoreline. All holes on this hilly (Scots would say undulating) course are challenging, but several are standouts. After a rather weak beginning at first which is a 219-yard par 4 whose only distinguishing feature is that it is straight uphill, get ready for a wild ride. Number seven, *Braes 'n' Dunes*, a 235-yard par 3, plays uphill more like 270 yards. *Auld Feartie*, the 208-yard, par 3 eleventh, is a demanding hole with a stone fence and forest left. What little fairway there is slopes severely right. On this hole Anne and I saw the largest hare we'd ever seen. It was so large that, at first, we thought it was a coyote, except Scotland doesn't have coyotes. It seemed like it was three feet tall when it was sitting! The next hole, *Clyde View*, a 314-yard par 4, provides a wonderful view of the Firth of Clyde and presents its own challenges. Your tee shot, ideally about 190 yards, must lay-up to the bottom of a fairly substantial, thick rough- and gorse-covered hill. The second shot is blind up the hill, but to a relatively open green. The Whiting Bay course finishes with a very strong last hole. *Springhill* is a 430-yard par 4 that's all downhill. Your second shot must land at least

30 yards short of the green; even in wet conditions the ball will run onto or through the swaled green. A small bar in the clubhouse may tempt you, just as they do throughout Isle Arran.

Sixteen miles from Whiting Bay, around the south end of the island and starting up the west coast, we find the "other" course I mentioned. As far as we are concerned, this is the highlight of Arran and one of the highlights of Scottish golf—**Shiskine Golf and Tennis Club** at Blackwaterfoot. What makes this an "other" is that it is a twelve-hole course. A few others exist in the world, but Shiskine is the oldest. In 1896 local golf enthusiasts recognized the Drumadoon *machair*, or farm, as prime golfing land similar to Scotland's other famous links courses. In 1896 Willie Fernie, the professional at Royal Troon, was commissioned to design a course at Blackwaterfoot. Only a couple of Fernie's original nine holes still exist—today's ninth and twelfth. In 1912 Musselburgh golf professional Willie Park was hired to complete the eighteen-hole course that had been hoped for. By May of 1913 the course was complete, with a major redesign of Fernie's nine and an additional nine, some of which were on hilly farmland next to the original course. Then came the war years of 1914 to 1918. The shorthanded membership found it difficult to maintain the new hill holes, so they were let to revert back to gorse and bracken. Once the war was over the club decided that the hill holes would be too difficult to maintain, and thus was born the world's first twelve-hole golf course. Many, who after playing the course, would say that Shiskine got it right; twelve holes is just about the correct number for holiday golf. But there is more that makes this course special than the number of holes. I once described this course to a friend as just an ordinary little linksland course with the Atlantic Ocean as a background, a covert cave used by Robert the Bruce as a hiding place before he united Scotland, and on the hill above the cave, a four-thousand-year-old Standing Stone. Just an ordinary little course! From every vantage point, Shiskine is special, and the golf is wonderful as well. The pro shop will provide the you with an information sheet telling about each hole. You will play better if you pay attention to the suggestions. Number three, *Crows Nest*, is a 135-yard par 3 that's absolutely blind. The tee shot must reach a plateaued green about 80 feet above the tee box. Use the signal flag here to let the tee know that you are still on the green. The very next hole is the spectacular *The Shelf*, a 144-yard par 3. From the most elevated spot on the course, you hit a shot down to a green backed by the Atlantic Ocean. It's a thrilling shot, especially with 30-mph winds ripping off the ocean directly into your face. The tee box of the fifth provides great views along the Kilbrannan Sound north to where the King's Cave can be found. One of my favorite holes (and on this course it's really hard to choose a favorite) is the 253-yard, par 4 eighth, called *Hades*. Your tee shot must clear bunkers, gorse, and heather to give you a shot at the fairly unprotected green. The fact that I lipped out an eagle chip from thirty yards the second time I played may have something to do with my affinity for this hole. After your round, visit the congenial tearoom near the clubhouse, where you can reflect about your round, rain or shine, on one of Scotland's best links courses.

While at Shiskine you might consider playing **Machrie Bay Golf Club,** about five miles north of Blackwaterfoot. Machrie Bay has a pleasant tearoom (hot and cold drinks, sandwiches, sweets) as part of the clubhouse, and some interesting holes. Machrie Bay is seaside golf, but not quite links golf. The tee box for the first hole is across the road from the clubhouse and the 262-yard hole plays with the Kilbrannan Sound on the right and the highway on the left. Need a straight tee shot here. Holes two through eight play on the inland side of the road and are fairly straightforward. Number nine, a 250-yard par 4, plays down to the highway, about 200 yards from the tee. The second shot must cross the road to find the green, about seven feet below the road level. Playing Shiskine in the morning and Machrie bay after a lunch break can make a glorious day of golf [see Chapter 10].

Leaving Isle Arran via the ferry that will take you from Lochranza at the north end of the island to Claonaig on the east coast of the Kintyre Peninsula, follow the B842 south toward Campbeltown. If you've driven this far in Scotland, you have no reason to fear this 17 mile stretch of single-track road. Pullouts and passing spots are plentiful, so that you can get around other (tourists), or to let others (locals) get around you. Just as the road begins to widen, and about the time you're ready for a break, the village of Carradale appears just a little off the main road (if a "B-road" can be called main). Here you find the little known **Carradale Golf Club**. This course is so out-of-the-way, we ran into many Scot golfers who didn't know about it. Built in the 1950s, this course, which overlooks the Kilbrannan Sound to the mountains of Arran, has been called "Kintyre's best kept secret." The nine-hole course offers interesting and challenging golf without bunkers. Rocky outcroppings and wild goats will keep the game interesting. And the people who play here seem to be some of the friendliest of Scottish golfers. We got help figuring out where to pay (at the honesty box in the men's changing room) and where the changing rooms were, and we were asked several times about our trip all before arriving at the first tee. The course, like many others in Scotland, is short, but has steep up and downs throughout. Anne really liked this course for the numerous elevated tee boxes. Number four, *Hillocks*, a 287-yard par 4, has one of those elevated tees. Your first shot is down to a broad fairway. The green is protected all around by heavy rough and uneven ground—so make the green or pay the penalty.

Pudding Bowl, the 289-yard, par 4 sixth plays again from an elevated tee. Your drive needs to stay away from the heavy rough on the left to have any hope of a easy second shot to the deep green. Number seven, *Port Righ*, is a 175-yard par 3 where your tee shot must clear several sections of deep rough. The views from here down to Carradale Bay are worth the price of admission. Shiskine and Carradale are quality short links courses, but they are only the opening acts.

The headliner on the Kintyre Peninsula is another twenty miles south to Campbeltown, and then six miles further west to the shores of Macrihanish Bay. Here you will find one of the two premier jewels of out-of-the-way Scottish Golf: the **Macrihanish Golf Club**. This golf club inspired architect Old Tom Morris to say in 1878, "The Almichty maun hae had gowf in his e'e when he made the place." Michael Bamberger in his 1992 book *To the Linksland*, likened Macrihanish to golf Nirvana. These aren't the only comparisons between Macrihanish and Heaven. If it weren't so out-of-the-way, Macrihanish would be on everyone's top-play list. Make the effort to play this outstanding eighteen-hole links course and you won't be disappointed. Another comment heard again and again is that the staff and members at Macrihanish are super-friendly. This is links golf, a Tom Morris course where accuracy off the tee is vital, as is proper clubbing to the well-maintained greens. As hard as it may be to select featured holes at a featured course, we have to give it a try. There's no better place to start a round of golf than the first hole at Macrihanish. It's a hole that draws universal praise. Tom Watson, five-time British Open Champion, has called it perhaps the best first hole in Scottish golf. It's a prime example of risk-reward golf. *Battery* is a 428-yard par 4 where the tee shot must cross the Atlantic Ocean if the tide is in or the Macrihanish beach if the tide is out. How much of the ocean/beach you choose to tackle is the risk; and the reward for a better shot is a shorter second shot. The second shot (length will depend upon how heavily you bailed on the first shot) must negotiate two fore bunkers to the otherwise unprotected green. A good start on this hole can make the rest of the round. Another of the strong holes is the ninth, *Ranachan*, a 353-yard par 4 that starts with a blind tee shot. The second shot must find a green protected by three pot bunkers left and one back. A hole that I particularly liked was number thirteen, *Kilkivan*, a 370-yard par four. It begins with a straight-away tee shot, but the second shot must carry the large cross bunker 50 yards from the back-sloping green, protected on both sides by pot bunkers. The course plays with only one par 3 on the front and no par 5s, and three par 3s and two 5s on the back. Macrihanish is links golf at its best: wind, rain, sun, ocean views, gorse, heather, rough, and bunkers, bunkers, bunkers.

One incident that pleased us at Macrihanish happened after the round. We played ahead of a local couple and we pulled further ahead as we went along. When we reached our car and were putting our clubs away before going into the clubhouse lounge, the couple we played ahead of came in and chatted with us in the parking lot. They commented about how fast we played "especially for Americans" and said, "You're welcome to come back anytime." Scots do expect and appreciate quick play.

Macrihanish may be a highlight to any Scotland golf trip, but the everyday community course can be fun as well. One year after staying in Oban (a seaside resort town, north on the A83 and A816 from Campbeltown and Macrihanish), we were looking for a quick golf stop as we headed toward Crieff and Central Scotland. Without knowing anything about it, we stopped for nine holes at **Dalmally Golf Club** (off A85 about 25 miles east of Oban). This is truly a community course; the members share in the groundskeeping duties. This is also an honesty box course where you sign in, leave your money in the box, and take your day ticket. Dalmally is a short parkland course with good views of surrounding hills, and where several holes follow the Orchy River. The most interesting hole on this pretty basic course is *Orchy Splash*, the 175-yard, par 3 third. The fairway doglegs around a bend in the river, and it takes either two shots or a big slice to reach the green from the tee. Or, for the adventurous, there's an opening right off the tee that gives you a straight shot to the green. Its about 160-yard carry to a small target. I'm sorry to say that I know why the hole has its name—twice! This is not high-class golf, but as one player said, "It's a nice inexpensive diversion if you're in the neighborhood."

From Ayr to Arran to Kintyre, all manner of exciting golf awaits. You can play the mountaintop or the *corrie* (Gaelic for "mountain hollow"), by the sea or in the sea (if you miss hit the first at Macrihanish). Wonderful out-of-the-way golf begs to be found here.

PUBS

Whether you seek refreshments or for a full meal in the the Ayr/Arran/Kintyre area, you have several choices. Fine lounges can be found at Belleisle and Macrihanish, as well as quaint tearooms at Corrie, Shiskine, and Machrie Bay. Culzean Castle has a cafe in their visitor centre, and Brodick Castle's tearoom offers some special ice cream dishes. But for this section, we selected eleven different sites which you ought to plan into your trip.

Our first recommendation is a sentimental favorite, as well as one we'd choose for its quality. For the past three years we've made our first

The A841, Isle Arran's main perimeter road, is both narrow and picturesque. The cemetery on the west side of the island is just known as the ancient graveyard.

The mountain views, from the green at the sixth hole at Corrie Golf Club, are spectacular (from left to right—Goat Fell Peak, Cir Mhor, and Caisteal Abhail).

The green on the first hole at Lamlash Golf Club affords a wondrous view of Holy Island in Lamlash Bay.

The Nether Largie Standing Stones, an arrangement of five stones with a lunar orientation, is just one of the many ancient monuments easily found in the Kilmartin valley south of Oban.

The sun setting over Kerrera Island is the view you have while enjoying a pint or a dram in Coasters Pub at Oban harbor.

Called the "Best First Shot in Scottish Golf," the tee shot on the 428-yard Battery at Macrihanish is a true risk/reward shot.

The sixth hole at Carradale Golf Club demonstrates the challenges which await on this hidden gem.

The friendly patrons and staff at Suie Lodge were happy to pose for a visitor, and had many interesting stories to tell.

night stay at a wonderful B&B in Alloway, next to Ayr (*Doonbrae,* owned by John and Moira Pollock-Morris). About an hour from the Glasgow airport, Alloway makes a good base for exploring the Ayrshire area and Robert Burns country. Directly across the street from *Doonbrae* is the **Brig o' Doon House Hotel**. This hotel opened in September of 1997, but looks like it has been here for many years. The hotel has five rooms to let, two restaurants and an upstairs lounge, and banquet facilities for 200 (in case you're traveling with a large group). The upstairs pub is set with comfortable stools and chairs around small tables. It's a great place for after-round conversation over a pint or dram and, even though food is available here, the dining rooms make a better choice. Decorated with fine art and tons of flowers and plants, the Brig o' Doon is classy and comfortable. Window seating is abundant in the two dining rooms, and the views of the River Doon and the *Auld Brig o' Doon* (the actual bridge) are straight out of Burns' tale, *Tam o' Shanter*. The evening menu is excellent, ranging from traditional Scottish dishes such as Haggis with Neeps and Tatties or Pan Fried Lamb Liver with Black Pudding, Smoked Bacon and Onion Sauce to standard fare like steak with peppercorn sauce. We've particularly enjoyed the soups (Mushroom and Tarragon, and a tasty Cullen Skink). One evening, salad special was Ham, Cheese & Tomato. After a long flight and a day of golf or touring, the Brig o' Doon House Hotel is a great choice for a relaxing drink and meal.

The Brig o' Doon House Hotel belongs to the Costley & Costley Hotel Group, which includes hotels in Prestwick, Troon, Kilmarnock, and Maidens (near Troon and Culzean Castle). It was to Maidens that we went for dinner after playing at Maybole and visiting Culzean Castle. In Maidens we found the **Wildings Hotel**. This new hotel and restaurant (2001) sits along the shore of Maidenhead Bay in the Firth of Clyde on the north side of the village (on A719). With a small bar area and two dining rooms, this is a busy eatery, and booking ahead would be wise. Wildings Hotel dining room is a modern, upscale seaside restaurant—bright and flashy without being garish. Lovely watercolor seascapes adorn the walls, at least in the room where we ate. The bar is very complete and is complimented by a good wine list. The menu is very strong on seafood (duh!) with unique dishes and a variety of sauces. The fish chowder was full of salmon and prawns and the Pan Fried Fish Medley consisted of generous portions of salmon, monkfish, brill, trout, cod and hake (a great sampler). The Wildings and Brig o' Doon aren't traditional pub fare establishments, but the prices were reasonable; they each had a bar you could eat in, and man or woman shouldn't have to live by pub grub alone. Besides, once we got to Isle Arran we found some great traditional pubs.

On Isle Arran we stayed at a fantastic B&B called Kilmichael's. It's the oldest house on the island, built on land granted by King Robert the Bruce in the 1300s. Its breakfast was wonderful and the dinners are legendary, but they are also very, very expensive. And since the price for the lodging was very high (almost twice that of Traquair House), Anne and I chose to find a good pub meal and save almost $100. In downtown Brodick we found the **Brodick Bar and Brasserie.** What a find! Across from the post office at the north end of the village, the pub here is modern, light, and airy with lots of windows. Ian McFadzean, the owner, told us that this section had been redesigned in the past year, but that there was a bit of history to the place. Even though it's been through several incarnations, it was still recommended by the Kilmichael staff. The building is over 40 years old, and Ian's father bought it about 25 years ago. The bar is still in the original bar building, and the brasserie section was first a house, then a pub-function room. The Brasserie, featuring light walls with dark-wood accents, has been the family serving area for about ten years. One of the best features of the Brasserie is the chalkboard menu, with its 30 to 40 color-coded items—starters, fish, beef, lamb, fowl, sweets. Food portions were very generous, and everything we've tried has been very outstanding. During one meal, we shared an excellent Mussels ala Marinara Soup, and ended with Sultana Sponge Pudding with Sauce Anglaise. This is a lively, friendly place where, over a tasty malt, we've compared golfing notes with people who played different courses. Brodick Bar and Brasserie is a place where we always like to stop.

On the more rustic side is the **Piershead Tavern** in Lamlash, just four miles south of Brodick. Could you guess that this tavern is directly across from the pier? The Piershead Tavern is a dark, beam-ceilinged, locals' pub with a stone bar and stonework walls. It's decorated with photos of the local area, and often plays its American 1960s pop music too loudly. But it's a friendly place with a full bar, a typical pub menu, and a couple of nightly specials thrown in. It's very self-service—order drinks and food at the bar or go thirsty and hungry. Two dogs in the pub both held their liquor well. The patrons are generally a mix of locals and tourists. The lasagna and the meat pie (specials for the night) were solid pub grub for a decent price, and the Guinness was, well, Guinness. Earlier in the day we'd played at Whiting Bay, another four miles down the road. It was fitting to end the day in a quaint, local pub. In the past year, the pub has sectioned off a room to make a more formal dining area.

On the shore of Whiting Bay is **The Pantry**, a small, bistro-style restaurant which is mostly windows overlooking the bay. A limited bar is supplemented by a reasonable wine list in this Scottish-Mexican restaurant. It's a busy place, even on week nights, so be sure to book ahead. The food is definitely worth it. The night we visited I had Guinness lamb stew and seafood enchiladas, and Anne had a goat cheese salad and teriyaki salmon stirfry. As upscale as the dinners were, the prices were decidedly pub prices.

For another quaint Isle Arran pub, try the village of Lagg at the south end of the island. Lagg and its close neighbor, Kilmory, are known for the Creamery nearby, which specializes in Arran Dunlop cheese, and the standing stones (*Torrylin Cairn*) a short hike away. In the village is a true public house built in 1791, **The Lagg Inn**. This tudor-style inn is decorated with pictures of the old hotel and region (c. 1850). A small bar stands at one end of the dining room, and it offers a limited selection of draughts but a better selection of malts (including Caol Ila, which is hard to find). A pub menu is provided for lunch, and a more extensive dinner menu for the evening in the Burnside Restaurant. We had tea and savory tomato soup. Anne, who's the tomato soup expert, said it was excellent, "Definitely not Campbell's." Even though this is a real public house, designed for people to visit on their way through, it's a place for the locals as well. While we were eating, I watched as a local came in, sat down, and rang a bell on the bar. The waitress came out and said, "The usual, Ted?" while she's already pouring him a Guinness. It's Cheers again. If the weather is cooperative, outside dining is available in garden overlooking the burn.

We have found many worthy pubs on Arran, certainly all those we mentioned. But perhaps the best is the **Catacol Hotel Pub** on the northwest side of the island, two miles from the ferry terminal at Lochranza. This is a simple country pub with a small bar made of big, old slabs of wood, and decorated with posters, promotions, and special menus. It has a surprisingly good selection of ales and malts for a small place. Catacol has an extensive pub menu with a half dozen specials, and serves from noon until 10:00 PM daily, with a buffet on Sunday. This isn't the high-tourist area Brodick is, so the trade is mostly local. As we were eating, a young girl stood at the bar in her fuzzy slippers reading the paper. The food we had at dinner was excellent: a creamed lentil soup followed by a generous portion of cod, chips, and mashed peas. Nothing fancy, just good food at a good price. The Catacol has been listed by some sources as the Best Pub on Arran. With traditional music sessions on Friday night, and trivia contests on Saturdays, we can see that this would be a lively place. It also had good rooms with wonderful views of the Kilbrannan Sound and Kintyre. A good bet for a before-dinner drink is to visit the Lochranza Distillery two miles north. The distillery provides an informative tour, a well-stocked gift shop, and the traditional complimentary dram at the end of the tour. The afternoon we stayed at Catacol Hotel, a lightning and thunder storm washed over the area; it drew everyone out of the pub to witness the show. We learned that an electrical storm is fairly rare in this area. After the storm blew over, Anne and I walked, across the street and onto the beach. A mild breeze, barely sweater weather, cooled us as we walked along the sound and watched seals and gulls in the gentle waves. Isle Arran is, indeed, Scotland in Miniature.

From Lochranza it's an easy half-hour ferry ride to Claonaig on the Kintyre Peninsula, but when you arrive, nothing is there. Claonaig is just a disembarking point. The destination from here is either north toward Oban or south to Campbeltown. We went south to play Carradale and Macrihanish, before heading north to Oban. In Campbeltown we found **MacGrochan's Bar** on the main street of town for lunch. MacGrochan's is a typical downtown pub, catering to business people, shoppers, and the occasional tourist. Decorated with with old alcohol posters (Cutty Sark, Tennets, Eagle Ale, etc.), MacGrochan's is a drinking place which serves food. The pub grub served was plentiful, Anne and I split a potato skin and bacon starter (Scottish bacon is similar to Canadian bacon) that was big enough for both our lunches when combined with a pint of Guinness. A poster proclaimed, "Guinness is food". The unique adornments in this pub are the posted signs. "Unsupervised children will be sold as slaves," caught our retired teachers' eyes first. As we looked around we found other interesting signs: "No swearing or blasphemy," "Food refusal will be punished," and "Strict silence at mealtimes." MacGrochan's made an enlightening lunch stop.

Oban (Gaelic for "little bay") is not necessarily golfer's paradise (though there is a reportedly good course, Glencruitten Golf Club, nearby, which we haven't yet played), but it is a tourist paradise. Queen Victoria called Oban, "One of the finest spots we have seen." This nice seaside community is home to several good eateries catering to the tourist population. One pub we like to stop at, especially for a drink, is **Coasters,** on the north end of the bay front (*Corran Esplanade*). This seaside pub serves food but its main attractions are the location and lively atmosphere. Nobody pays much attention to the beer ad decor. The small tables and chairs are easily rearranged to fit the group, while on Friday night it's hard to find a spot and difficult to hear over the loud jukebox. There were a few locals and lots of holiday crowd, even late in the season. We chatted with a group of visiting seniors who were beginning a pub crawl, their first stop being Coasters. The main attraction at coasters is location, location, location—that and the sunsets over Oban Bay.

A second locale to visit in Oban (also on the *Esplanade*) is the 1790 historic harborside pub, **The Oban Inn.** You can feel the age in this upstairs, pub with its dark wood ceilings, booths, and captain's chair bar stools. A nice touch is the real fireplace with a peat fire that gave a pleasant aroma to the room. The small bar has a broad selection of malts, including all the Glenmorangie selections, several Bowmore, and some rarer examples of the distiller's art. This is a better choice for food than Coasters, but it's still only a decent bar menu. There are many fine dining places in Oban, though most are a bit pricey. The food was good, but basic—we had a cumberland sausage and mash, and a haddock and chips. The Oban Inn is a quaint, friendly, historic pub; a pleasing place for a quick meal and a dram.

A last stop on this leg of our tour around Scotland is on the A85, the main road between Oban and central Scotland. About eight miles north of the head of Loch Lomond, Crianlarich is a staging area for transportation routes. The railway splits here, roads converge, and even The West Highland Way long distance footpath passes. But little else draws the visitor. So, when we drove through on our way from Oban to Crieff one year, we were unsuccessful finding food. This place didn't serve meals, and the next one had already stopped serving lunch. We were lucky, (and hungry), though, when we stopped at **Suie Lodge Hotel** in Glen Dochart east of Crianlarich. Owners Peter and Betty Shoulders and Vicky Hunter serve food all day at this hunting lodge. History abounds at here. The business began life as a private hunting lodge on the Breadalbane Estate, then it became a family home, and finally about 40 years ago, it was turned into a hotel. The lodge itself is listed as a building of architectural and historical interest. Across the road from the lodge is an ancient Clan MacNab burial site, marked by a stone which is engraved with a Latin cross. It is thought that the stone may date to St. Fillan, who had his seat (*suie* is Gaelic for *seat*) of learning at this place. St. Fillan's Bell (*Bearnan Fillan*) was at Suie and now resides in the Scottish National Museum of Antiquities. Peter and Betty have an interesting history here as well. Until a few years ago they were both British space scientists who, when they tired of the rat race, sought a quieter lifestyle. They found it at Suie Lodge Hotel, and they love the choice they made. We had a late lunch in the pub area, separate from the formal dining area, decorated with game pictures, antlers, and antique pistols. The pub menu was typical, but several daily specials are offered. Anne and I tried two of the specials—venison casserole and wild game pie. Both were homemade and delicious. Suie Lodge Hotel caters to hunters, fishermen, and hikers, but tourists planning to be in the area or pass through should consider a stop here for the food, the history, and the stories.

ATTRACTIONS

As we consider the sites and activities in the Ayr-Arran-Kintyre area, it's easiest to follow the same path as the golfing tour and the pub tour. We'll explore the Ayrshire area, then travel to Isle Arran, and finally visit the Kintyre peninsula up to Oban.

The biggest attraction on the Ayrshire coast is the spectacular **Culzean Castle and Country Park,** located eight miles south of Ayr on A719. Culzean (pronounced "cullayne") is the former Kennedy estate castle which famed Scottish neoclassical architect Robert Adams redesigned at the end of the 18th Century. The setting is awe-inspiring, as the castle hangs on the cliffs overlooking the Firth of Clyde and Isle Arran. The National Trust for Scotland, which was given control of the castle in 1945, provides very informative tours of its interior (although you can self-tour). The most striking feature of Culzean is the Oval Staircase which is Adams' finest work and is supported by three tiers of columns. At the top of the staircase you visit the Saloon used for entertaining. The ceiling was restored to its original colors in 1968 after some original drawings were found hidden away. This is a wonderful example of 18th Century elegance. Be sure to look out the windows of the Saloon at the 150-foot drop to the rocks and breakers of the Firth. Rooms are full of treasures here, including china and porcelain, and early-19th Century weapons. One of the most interesting features of Culzean is the upper-floor apartment, which was given to General Dwight David Eisenhower in thanks for his leadership in World War II. The Eisenhower Apartment was visited by Ike and Mrs. Eisenhower four times. Today, the apartment is available as a rental for about $500 a night. The castle tour will take about an hour, and you can spend at least that long wandering the grounds. Flower gardens, a forest trail, a battery, and much more are on display. Look closely at unique designs on the cannons in the courtyard and side yard. Something else that makes Culzean unique is that the 565-acre grounds were accepted in 1970 as Scotland's first Country Park. The last stop on a tour of the Castle grounds should be the Visitor's Centre, with gift shop and tearoom.

About three miles to the east on A77 we visited a most fascinating ruin. **Crossraguel Abbey**, built in 1244 as a Clunic Monastery (one of only two in Scotland), has several parts still in good condition. The name Crossraguel comes from *The Cross of Riaghail*, an early-Christian prayer cross which was probably in the area. The Tower House is mostly complete with good views of the surrounding countryside from the upper-floor windows. The Sacristy is also in good repair with quite a few mason marks visible and some interesting acoustics to the room. Finally, walk across the main yard to the *doocot* (dovecot or dove house). This *doocot*, built in the 16th Century, is one of the oldest in Scotland. Here doves or pigeons were kept as in a larder or early Scottish refrigerator. You only had to step in to grab an egg or two or a fresh bird for the dinner table.

The last of the Ayrshire attractions we want to suggest you visit isn't in one place. **Robert Burns Country** is all throughout the area. Robert Burns, Scotland's national poet (who penned *Ode to a Haggis* and *Auld Lang Syne*), was born in Alloway in the mid-18th Century (1759-1784). His birth house, the **Burns Cottage,** built by Robert's father William Burns, is only a three-wood shot away from Belleisle Golf Club. The Cottage demonstrates the living conditions of the tenant farmer family, and has next to it a small museum and peaceful gardens. The **Burns Monument,** with another small museum and gardens, is down the road and across from both Brig o' Doon House Hotel and the **Alloway Kirkyard,** where much of the famous Burns' tale *Tam O' Shanter* takes place. Further afield, in the village of Kirkoswald about 14 miles south of Ayr (A77) is **Souter Johnnies' Cottage** (*souter* meaning *cobbler*). The cottage is the real house of John Davidson, a companion to Robert Burns, who ended up as a character in the *Tam o' Shanter* poem. The cottage furnishings (c. 1790) provides a good contrast to the Burns Cottage. The Davidson cottage displays how much better a tradesman would have lived than the farmer Burns. Ayrshire may be the center of Burns Country, but throughout Scotland will be found reference to the famous poet and songwriter—a real son of Scotland.

North on the Ayrshire coast is the ferry terminal town of Androssan. Here is where you board the Caledonian MacBrayne Ferries to the western islands, and particularly Isle Arran. The 45-minute ferry ride is bookable online, or tickets can be purchased at the the the ferry terminal. In summer it's advisable to pre-book, as the ferry traffic is heavy. Watching the ferry load the rest of the vehicles after we drove our car on was very interesting. Early cars were elevated into decks above the main floor, and later trucks had to back down the gangway into the ferry interior. Passengers have several options for the trip, including spending time in the bar, coffee shop, observation lounge, outside decks, or all of the above. Not being a very seafaring person, I enjoyed the outside deck and watching the approach to the island. A small pair of travel binoculars comes in very handy. On one of our trips we met several friendly dogs (and their owners), heading over to Arran for some holiday time. The ferry arrives on Arran at the main village of the island, Brodick.

In the village are several hotels or guesthouses, various kinds of shops, a market, and at the edge of town is the Brodick Golf Club. Just about a mile north of town on the main island road are two places to stop: **Arran Aromatics** and the **Island Cheese Company**. Arran Aromatics opened in 1997 and sells a range of about 300 soaps and lotions, all made with island ingredients. It's not really my kind of place, but Anne loves to shop there for herself and for gifts to take home. She says that they sell some special combinations (honey-and-orange-blossom hand lotion is one she loves), and everyone who buys products from Arran Aromatics loves them. While she shops there, I go next door to the Island Cheese Company factory and store to watch as they hand-dip cheese rounds. Here we stock up on cheese for lunches out on the golf course. Cheese and scones or biscuits makes a great, light snack after the huge Scottish breakfasts we eat in B&Bs. Island Cheese Co. specializes in flavored cheddars, Arran Blue, and crowdies (a type of white cheese) with toasted oatmeal coatings.

A half mile farther north is **Brodick Castle**, the home of the Hamiltons since 1503. The castle overlooks Brodick Bay and the Firth of Clyde, while behind it stands Goatfell Peak, the tallest point on the island at 2866 feet. Brodick Castle is a fine example of a Victorian Highland Estate with library, drawing room, dining room, boudoir, and several other rooms open for visitors. The entrance hall has an impressive display of 87 red deer stag's heads that were shot on the island in earlier times. A thriving population of red deer still inhabits the island. The Walled Garden, created in 1710, and 65 acres of Woodland Gardens were gorgeous in early September; and the Rhododendron Gardens (best in April to mid-June) are touted to be the finest in Scotland. Brodick Castle, with its island location, is another fascinating castle to visit in Scotland.

Brodick Castle may only be 500 years old, but even older antiquities dot in the area. Isle Arran and the Kintyre Peninsula are rich with **Standing Stones, Stone Circles, and Pictish Stones**. These are the relics of early settlers to Scotland, many of whom have histories nearly lost to the ages. Much of the stonework left by ancient people has been lost, but Scotland has done a painstaking job protecting and preserving what remains. On our way around Isle Arran we visited many sites to look at various stones and cairns. At Torrylin in the south (near Kilmory), at Machrie Moor (near Blackwaterfoot), Auchagallon, and Moss Farm (both on the west side), we found excellent examples of Bronze Age stone circles and cairns (burial mounds), dating to about 1500 BC (almost as old as Stonehenge). These monuments served various functions, religious or astronomical, in the lives of the early inhabitants. The best sites, though, are along A816 between Tarbert and Oban. Throughout the Kilmartin Glen can be found some of mainland Scotland's most important prehistoric sites. Most important is the

Linear Cemetery, a more-than-two-mile alignment of stones and cairns thought to indicate burial grounds for an important family or chieftain. When we first toured this area, we stopped at a site that had a burial cairn and a set of large standing stones in a sheep field. We didn't understand what we were seeing until we visited the **Museum of Ancient Culture** in Kilmartin. The museum is informational and entertaining, with video presentations, as well as hands-on exhibits which help explain various theories about the area's prehistoric sites. If the weather is decent and it's been dry, stop to see **Dunadd Fort**, an Iron Age fort occupying the top of a 175 foot hill. Several interesting stone carvings are at Dunadd, and a wonderful view can be enjoyed from the top, though the climb can be very slippery if it's wet. I've got the stained and torn pants to prove it. If you don't have time, or the weather is too inclement to wander the fields looking at archeological sites, be sure to stop at the museum in Kilmartin and visit the church next door, which houses many relics.

Not far from either Kilmartin or Oban is **Arduaine Gardens** (about 10 miles north of Kilmartin and 18 miles south of Oban on A816). These small gardens enjoy a serene, lochside setting, with views of Asknish Bay and the islands of Shuna, Luing, Scarba, and Jura. The gardens are most prolific in early summer (May and June), but are worth a visit at other times as well. Rhoddies and azaleas predominate, but the forest walk is enjoyable just for itself. It's a pleasant place to pause, and the Loch Melfort Hotel next to the gardens is a picturesque place for a snack or a pint.

Before telling you about the most special attraction in this western area, we'd suggest another castle stop. In a suburb of Oban at the mouth of Loch Etive lie the impressive ruins of **Dunstaffnage Castle**. The 13th Century seat of Clan MacDougalls, Dunstaffnage Castle has huge, curtain-wall battlements, to a large extent still intact. A chapel is set in the woods by the castle, as well. This is worth a visit, if only for the views of the castle exterior and loch.

As beautiful as Culzean is, as impressive as Dunstaffnagen is, as intriguing as the stone circles are, the trip to Iona is more beautiful, more impressive, and more intriguing. This side trip begins in the seaside town of **Oban**. Oban makes a convenient base for exploring **Mull** and **Iona.** Interesting shopping, quality restaurants and pubs, and historically significant sites are found in Oban. Try to leave some time to visit McCraig's Tower (also called McCraig's Folly), an imitation of the Roman Coliseum that was financed by a local businessman as a make-work project. Also plan to drop by the Oban Distillery for an informative tour which ends with the traditional dram of the local product. One of Oban's main functions now is as a ferry terminal for ships heading to the Scottish western islands of Mull, Jura, Islay, and Harris and Lewis. It is also the starting point for the exploration of Scotland's most holy site—**the Isle of Iona**. Only three miles long and not even a mile wide, Iona lies less than half a mile off the southern point of the island of Mull. Iona has been a place of Christian worship since the 600s, and is today a place of Christian pilgrimage. To reach Iona, Anne and I booked a tour with Bowman's Tours in Oban; including ferry passage from Oban to Mull, a bus tour from Craignure to Fionnphort (on Mull), ferry passage to Iona, and return to Oban. The half-hour ferry trip from Oban to Mull furnishes marvelous views of Oban harbor, Dunollie Castle (ruins just outside of Oban), and Duart Castle on Mull (home of Clan MacLean). Our bus tour was interesting with Michael, a 27 year resident of Mull, as our guide,. We learned a good bit about the history and geology of Mull on the hour trip to Fionnphort. We also learned a lot about driving from Michael, as he negotiated the 37 miles of single-track road. At Fionnphort we boarded a smaller ferry (passengers and six cars) for the ten-minute ride to Iona. It was telling that the ferry limit was 250 in the summer, but only 50 in the winter months. Once we landed in Iona at Baile Mor (the only village on the island), all the features were within walking distance. We had three hours to explore Iona, just enough time to get a feel for the history here. The three major attractions on the island are the **Nunnery, St. Oran's Chapel, and the Abbey**. Iona is where St. Columba (*Colum Cille*), coming from Ireland, established a Celtic Christian settlement, from which missionaries converted the rest of Britain. Today the ruins of the 11th Century Augustinian Nunnery are well preserved as a nice garden. Farther down the road (the only one on Iona) is St. Oran's Chapel and the Graveyard of Kings. In this graveyard (*Reilig Odhrain*) are buried the remains of 60 kings of Norway, France, Ireland, and Scotland. King Duncan and King MacBeth are both rumored to be buried here. The Abbey itself, built in the 13th Century and enlarged in the 15th, is still in use as a nondenominational house of worship and for religious retreats. Visitors, regardless of their religious backgrounds, cannot fail to be impressed by this sacred ground. On our way to catch the return ferry, we found a curious little bookstore with a wide selection of used books on Scottish history. Iona is a locus for the spirit and the intellect.

Exploring Ayr, Isle Arran, the Kintyre Peninsula and Oban, Mull, and Iona takes more than just a couple of days. This area possesses a wealth of challenging and unique golf, and plenty of fine eating and drinking establishments. This area is also rich in historical sites. A visitor could easily plan to spend a week or two.

GOLF COURSE INFORMATION

Course: **Belleisle Golf Club**
Style & Length: Parkland, 6431 yds, par 72
Price: 20GBP
Availability: Busy course, check in advance
Phone: (01292) 441258
Web: www.golfsouthayrshire.com/belleisle

Course: **Seafield Golf Club**
Style & Length: Links/Parkland, 5498 yds, par 66
Price: 14GBP
Availability: Easy to get on
Phone: (01292) 441258
Web: www.golfsouthayrshire.com/seafield

Course: **Maybole Municipal Golf Club**
Style & length: Parkland, 2635 yds, par 33
Price: Very inexpensive
Availability: Welcome anytime, limited trolleys
Phone: (01655) 889770
Web: ww.golfsouthayrshire.com/maybole

Course: **Doon Valley Golf Club**
Style & Length: Inland, 2943 yds, par 34
Price: 10GBP/18 holes
Availability: Easy to get on
Phone: (01292) 531607

Course: **Corrie Golf Club**
Style & Length: Heathland, 1948 yds, par 31
Price: 10GBP/day
Availability: Welcome except Sat. PM, no trolleys
Phone: (01770) 810223

Course: **Lamlash Golf Club**
Style & Length: Parkland hilly, 4640 yds, par 64
Price: 16GBP
Availability: Fairly easy to get on
Phone: (01770) 600296
Web: www.lamlashgolfclub.co.uk

Course:	**Whiting Bay Golf Club**
Style & Length:	Heathland hilly, 4405 yds, par 63
Price:	15GBP
Availability:	Welcome after 9:30 AM
Phone:	(01779) 700487

Course:	**Shiskine Golf and Tennis Club**
Style & Length:	Links, 2990 yds 12 holes, par 42
Price:	15GBP
Availability:	Very popular, but only reserves 24 hours ahead during July and August, two rounds per day limit
Phone:	(01770) 860226
Web:	www.shiskinegolf.com

Course:	**Machrie Bay Golf Club**
Style & Length:	Parkland/Links, 2220 yds, par 33
Price:	8GBP/day
Availability:	Welcome anytime
Phone:	(01770) 850232

Course:	**Carradale Golf Club**
Style & Length:	Links w/o bunkers, 2392 yds, par 32
Price:	10GBP/day
Availability:	Just show up
Phone:	(01583) 431378

Course:	**Macrihanish Golf Club**
Style & Length:	Links, 6228 yds, par 71
Price:	30GBP
Availability:	No restrictions
Phone:	(01586) 810213
Web:	www.macgolf.com

Course:	**Dalmally Golf Club**
Style & Length:	Parkland, 2257 yds, par 31
Price:	10GBP/day (honesty box)
Availability:	Anytime, restricted Sundays, no trolleys
Phone:	(01838) 200370
Web:	www.loch-awe.com/golfclub

Chapter Ten:
The Best of Scotland

A GREAT DAY IN SCOTLAND

During our six trips to Scotland we have experienced no bad days. But describing a full day might prepare you for what to expect during your own golf trip. Monday, September 8, 2003, was our only full day on Isle Arran, off the west coast of Scotland between Ayrshire and the Kintyre Peninsula.

I arose early and took a morning walk in the village of Lamlash, where our B&B, Lilybank House, was located. As I meandered along, quaint village cottages and shops caught my eye on one side of the road, and Lamlash Bay, filled with moored pleasure boats and a couple of commercial fishing trawlers adorned the other. Holy Island sparkled in the early morning sunlight. Along my walk I met Colin Richardson, our B&B host, walking his dog. Colin sarcastically apologized for the weather which was sunny and about 15 degrees Celsius, and windless. In other words, Fantastic! Colin had also "apologized" the night before for the poor view from our room—a splendid view directly out to the bay and Holy Island. Back from my walk, having taken a couple dozen photos of the bay, the boats in the bay, Holy Island, houses, flowers, and the kirk (church), I went with Anne down to breakfast at 8:30.

Colin served a well-prepared, typical Scottish breakfast: various cereals, fruit, fruit juices, coffee or tea, Canadian-style bacon, bangers, eggs, potatoes, grilled mushrooms and tomatoes, and all the toast we wanted. It's your own fault if you go hungry in a Scottish B&B. After breakfast we packed our stuffed bellies into our rented, valiant Vauxhall Vector and headed for golf.

Isle Arran has a main road around the perimeter of the island (A841), and a lesser road (B880), which bisects the island from the main village of Brodick on the east to Blackwaterfoot on the west. It's this cross-island route we took to make our tee time at Shiskine Golf and Tennis Club. The B880 afforded wonderful views as we headed up the 700-foot pass. The views of Goat Fell peak (the island's highest at 2868 feet) and surrounding mountains was complemented with vistas of the ocean and Kintyre Peninsula beyond.

Shiskine is unique in the golfing world. It's a twelve-hole links course which plays along the Kilbrannan Sound. Built on ancient sand dunes, Shiskine has enough scenery to make any golfer miss shots. Besides the sound and the peninsula, there are stunning cliffs, home to a myriad of seabirds. Anne's golf was good, and while my swing was off, it would be hard to have a bad golf day in such a beautiful place.

After golf we grabbed a couple of Cokes at the tearoom and headed up the coast to a beach pullout a couple of hundred yards past the Machrie Bay GC clubhouse. We sat on the shore and shared a light lunch of oatcakes (crackers), Arran smokey cheddar cheese, and enjoyed our Cokes. Refreshed by the sea air and our snacks, we drove back to Machrie Bay GC to play nine more holes. This course has some interesting features: Hole one plays between the main Arran road and the beach, you cross the road to play holes 2 through 8, nine crosses the road again when you shoot to the green, a standing stone (probably 1500 BC) dominates the sheep field next to #3, and from several holes you can see the Auchagallen Stone Circle (older than the Pyramids). Other than that it's just an average, nine-hole course.

With 21 holes of golf complete, we continued up the coast, making a couple of photo stops (an interesting graveyard; quaint, narrow roads), and for Anne to go down to the beach and collect stones, which she hides in our luggage to bring home, and which I pretend not to notice. At the tip of the island we reach Lochranza, with its 15th Century castle and whisky distillery. We take pictures of the castle, but we visit the distillery. Visitors to Scotland cannot live by haggis alone!

Up the west side of Isle Arran, at the ferry terminal town of Lochranza at the north tip of the island, the road swings east to the village of Corrie, and then south toward Brodick. [I think I get bonus points for using all four compass points in one grammatically correct sentence.] Before we reach Brodick we stop at Island Cheese Shop and Arran Aromatics, where Anne stocks up on soaps, lotions, and wonderfully smelly girl goo. In Brodick I stock up on wonderfully smelly, rich-tasting sweets at Arran Chocolates. To each his/her own.

We arrive back at Lillybank House with time enough to taste some of our purchases. We sit in our room overlooking the bay, sipping whisky and nibbling cheese and chocolates. At our request, Colin has booked us into The Pantry—a Scottish-Mexican bistro in Whiting Bay about seven miles away. At The Pantry we enjoy Lamb Guinness Soup and seafood enchiladas with mornay sauce. A delicious and unique meal, eaten while watching the water lap at Whiting Bay.

It's 9:30 by the time we get back to Lamlash. We just have time to organize the day's souvenirs and purchases in our bags and write in journals—travel journal, golf notes, and pub notes. We both fall asleep reading, but that's okay, we need to rest because tomorrow we play golf at Corrie in the morning, and catch the ferry back to the terminal at Ardrossan at noon, and drive on to Crieff in Central Scotland.

Another great day in Scotland.

MY TOP TEN OUT OF THE WAY GOLF COURSES

In each chapter, we've described the out-of-the-way golf courses we've played during six golfing trips. We've omitted the famous courses we've played—the Turnberrys, the Royal Troons, the Old Course. We've also left out the few courses we think it best to avoid. What we haven't done is present a listing of the courses we most enjoyed. To do that, I will order my ten favorite courses, and then Anne will do the same for her top five ladies' courses. Remember, like everything else in this book, our choices are subjective. They're our lists. With that caveat, I present my favorite hidden gems of Scottish golf:

10. Silloth on Solway GC, Silloth, England.
As good as Southerness and Powfoot are on the Scotland side of the Solway Firth, I like Silloth better. Generous fairways and tough bunkers make Silloth an enjoyable test (and to a former   teacher that's important). The views of the firth are stunning.

9. Crail Balcomie Links, Fife.
The age and history of the course is part of the draw. For me it is the combination of first playing the great links holes and then strolling around a point to finish with some tough parkland holes. Some people may not like the change in the last four holes, but I see it as an added attraction. It's like getting two courses in one.

8. North Berwick West Links, East Lothian.

Some may be surprised that I would place one of the most famous courses, an Open-qualifying venue, so low on my list of favorites. North Berwick is a great course I would go back to any chance I get, but others are even better.

7. Murrayshall GC, Perthshire.

Murrayshall is one of the best parkland courses I've ever played. Wonderful views combine here with great holes. I can picture vividly the par-three eighth where the tee shot is down a narrowing tunnel of trees to the small, partially hidden green. Stunning parkland golf.

6. Macrihanish, Kintyre.

Beautiful links golf with an absolutely world-class first shot over the Atlantic. I've played the course only once and feel it might move up on my list if I had played it more. Its isolation is its attraction and its drawback.

5. Fortrose and Rosemarkie, Black Isle.

So much draws me to the course—the challenging holes, the views of the Firth of Moray, the history of golf on the land, and the history of the linksland it's built upon. We definitely plan our Scotland golf trips around playing Fortrose.

4. St. Fillans, near Crieff.

To me this is the quintessential, small-village golf course. The setting is drop-dead gorgeous, the holes are easy enough to be fun, yet difficult enough to keep me thinking, the staff and club   members are friendly, and the tearoom has great homemade sweets. Not much more to want in Scottish golf.

3. Boat of Garten, Highlands.

What's not to like about Boat? It's tough (rough, bunkers, trees, elevation changes, tricky greens) and it is fair. Hit it well at Boat and you get rewarded. Hit off-line and pay the price. Length helps, but accuracy is more important. The setting is stupendous, filled with mountain and river views, birch forests, and a steam train chugging beside the course. After you finish a round at Boat the clubhouse has a great lounge for a malt, a meal, or a brew.

2. Royal Dornoch, Highlands.
Truly championship golf as tough as it can be and still be playable by the average player. Prettiest in the spring and early summer when the broom and gorse bloom brightly yellow, the course is always lovely and wonderfully conditioned. Players like Tom Watson aren't wrong when they say that Royal Dornoch may be the best out-of-the-way test of your golf skills in the world.

1. Shiskine, Blackwaterfoot, Isle Arran.
If I could play   only one course for the rest of my days, it would be Shiskine Golf and Tennis Club. Twelve holes is a very good number and twenty-four (two rounds) is not bad either. Every hole at Shiskine is so different that it makes a round seem unbelievably full. The views are unrivaled and the golf challenging— I always feel that birdies and bogies or worse are real possibilities on every hole. I have found no better golfing adventure anywhere.

ANNE'S PICK FOR THE LADIES

What I might like in a golf course, Anne may not. I don't mind a carry over gorse or water, as long as it's not too severe. Anne gets bothered even if the carry is well within her range. I prefer nice views on a golf course, while Anne often measures the quality of a course solely by its views. All this means that Anne has a list of favorite Scottish courses which differs from mine. Here's her randomly ordered list of courses, one Anne believes will appeal to women golfers in her handicap range of 23 to 26:

Fortrose and Rosemarkie, Black Isle.
Very pretty with great sea views. Easy to score well by playing down the middle.

Boat of Garten, Highlands.
Easy-to-walk with nice forest views and a quaint steam train which chugs beside the course. Very fair for straight hitters.

North Berwick West, East Lothian.
A very difficult course, yet fun. Stretching along the Firth of Forth with views of Bass Rock, the course is a real beauty. Even in heavy wind and rain, the course was a joy to play.

Tain, Highlands.
Similar in style to Royal Dornoch, Tain is easier to play with fewer funny bounces. Beautiful holes and great vistas.

Shiskine, Blackwaterfoot, Isle Arran.
I was wrong! Anne did pick her favorite, Shiskine. With Kilbrannan Sound, the Kintyre Peninsula, and the towering sea cliffs of Drumadoon Point visible from every hole, you'll find no more lovely place to play golf. The course is full of tricky, but fair shots. For instance, the par-3 third has an unreachable (for Anne) plateaued green, but a bailout area awaits her halfway to the green. Two good short iron shots and she has as much chance of making par as I do. She's usually on the green while I'm still trying to find my ball in the rough. The bottom line is that whether or not she's played well, she walks off the course saying, "Can we come back tomorrow?"

STOP FOR A BITE OR A BREW

In these chapters we've mentioned more than fifty pubs, restaurants, or bistros. We believe that they are all good enough to recommend to our friends. Which ones would we choose as the best? After much discussion, rereading notes and journals, and wracking our memories, we've come up with a list of special recommendations.

Best Golfer's Pub:
1. Eagle Hotel, Dornoch
2. Old Aberlady Inn

Best Seafood:
1. Bunnillidh Restaurant, Helmsdale
2. Creel Inn, Catterline

Best Pub Menu:
1. Brodick Brasserie, Isle Arran
2. Old Aberlady Inn

Best Location:
1. Tormaukin Hotel, Glen Devon
2. Loch Tummel Inn, Loch Tummel

Best Beers:
1. Moulin Inn, near Pitlochry (Moulin Brewery)
2. Traquair Arms, Innerleithen (Traquair Ales)

Most Historic:
1. Dreel Tavern, Anstruther
2. Brig O' Doon House Hotel, Alloway

Best Golf Course Tearoom:
1. Killin GC, Killin
2. St. Fillans GC, St. Fillans

Best Golf Course Clubhouse Pub:
1. Royal Dornoch, Dornoch
2. Fortrose & Rosemarkie GC, Fortrose

THREE TEN-DAY OUT-OF-THE-WAY SCOTLAND ITINERARIES

Several of our non-golfing friends have asked us where they should go on their trips to Scotland. We try to help them design a trip they would enjoy. What would we recommend, though, if someone wanted to take an out-of-the-way golf tour of Scotland? Anne and I discussed whether to go north or south, to Arran, or to the Fife. In the end, we couldn't put together just one trip; instead, we designed three ten-day itineraries.

When weighing these itineraries, keep in mind several considerations:

- You must realize that to travel ten days in Scotland really takes twelve days. From the States, especially the west coast, you lose one day each way to travel.

- When we travel, we like to stay busy on our arrival day. Not only does it extend our trip, but by staying up until at least 9:00 PM, it helps us to adjust to Scottish time.

- We have yet to recommend any lodgings in the golf chapters because it seemed too big a task. But on these itineraries we've included some of the B&Bs and small guesthouse hotels we've liked.

- You'll notice that we try to stay in one place for two or three days at a time. One-night stays are often a travel necessity, but it is much less stressful to stay in the same locale at least for a couple of days.

- We suggest staying the last night in an airport hotel to make catching the early flight easier the next day. By staying at the airport that last night, we can have the car returned and our flights checked the day before we fly. If there are any problems, and there have been, we have time to deal with them before a 6:00 AM flight.

The following, then, are three trips with emphasis on the hidden gems of Scottish golf.

TRIP ONE:
CENTRAL, NORTH, AND THE FIFE

Day One: *Arrive in Glasgow or Edinburgh about midday (pick whichever gives you the best fares or flights). Pick up your rental car and, after some practice driving around the parking lot, drive to Crieff.*

> **Golf:** Nine holes at the Crieff Dornoch course.
> **Where to Stay:** We suggest a B&B like Merlindale or a small guesthouse like Arduthie House Hotel.
> **Where to Eat:** Dinner at a local pub (Arduthie, Haggis & Sporran, or Meadow Inn).

Day Two: *Stay in the area after golf, and explore Drummond Castle Gardens or Famous Grouse Experience (Glenturret Distillery).*

> **Golf:** Eighteen holes at the Crieff Ferntower course.
> **Where to Stay:** Same as day one.
> **Where to Eat:** If staying at a B&B which serves dinner, like Merlindale, try to arrange a B&B dinner.

Day Three: *Start your trip north with golf and stay in Pitlochry, where you can shop, or drive the few extra miles to Edradour Distillery.*

> **Golf:** Play eighteen holes at one of the Murrayshall courses, just outside of Perth before you head up the A9.
> **Where to Stay:** Stay at either the Moulin Hotel a mile from town, or try an in-town, golfer-friendly (we met the host on the golf course) B&B like Dundarave House.
> **Where to Eat:** Have dinner at the Moulin Inn and be sure to sample their brews.

Day Four: *Continue the trip north with golf on the way.*

> **Golf:** Eighteen holes at Boat of Garten GC a few miles east of the A9, about half way to tonight's destination in the village of Dornoch.

Out for a morning walk, I look back to get a picture of the village of Lamlash from the other side of the bay.

Between rounds of golf, Anne and I stopped for lunch on a beach just north of Machrie Bay Golf Club. As we nibbled our bread and cheese, we looked across the Kilbrannan Sound to the Kintyre Peninsula.

While Anne shops at Arran Aromatics, I watched the cheese-maker at Island Cheese Co. dipping rounds into wax.

One of our two picks for Best Beer, the Moulin Hotel near Pitlochry, is a wonderful dinner location with interesting specials each night.

The 403-yard sixth, called Avenue, is characteristic of the fine heathland holes found at my third-favorite out-of-the-way course in Scotland, Boat of Garten.

The gaping bunkers at the fourth hole on Royal Dornoch are both the challenge and the charm on this championship links course.

Shiskine Golf and Tennis Club represents the best of out-of-the-way golf courses in Scotland. The view here is of the fourth green, Drumadoon Head, and the Kilbrannan Sound.

The Dreel Tavern in Anstruther is a 17th Century coaching inn which still serves fine meals and a good draught. It's one of our best picks for historic pubs.

Where to Stay: In Dornoch, stay at either the Eagle Hotel or Mallin House Hotel. Both are functional golfer's hotels with decent food. Many B&Bs are in the area, but we haven't stayed at any.

Where to Eat: Try dinner at the Sutherland House or at the hotel pubs.

Day Five: A day for championship golf, and either a visit to Glenmorangie Distillery or a second round at the Dornoch Struie course.

Golf: Enjoy a wonderful round on Royal Dornoch, one of golf's great courses (tee time should be arranged in advance via web).

Where to Stay: Same as day four

Where to Eat: Try one of the eateries you didn't select last night.

Day Six: Begin the trip east and south.

Golf: Either play eighteen at Dornoch again (you can never play that course too often), or travel a few miles south and play Tain GC or Fortrose GC.

Where to Stay: There are many B&Bs in Nairn on the Moray Firth that can be booked via the web.

Where to Eat: Ask your B&B hosts for a recommendation. We've hardly ever been given bad advice, especially if we let them know what we like.

Day Seven: The trip is winding down, but there is still plenty of adventure awaiting as we head south toward the Fife. On the way, today, will be an exciting drive over the Highlands, and many chances to visit castles like Craigievar.

Golf: Play a course on the Moray Firth—Nairn Dunbar or Hopeman would be good choices.

Where to Stay: We would suggest Stonehaven rather then Aberdeen, but then we're biased toward the small towns. There are good B&Bs in Stonehaven, but the one we've always stayed at is now for sale, so we'll start looking for a new one.

Where to Eat: There are several good choices in town, but if you don't mind driving small roads, go to Catterline's Creel Inn (quality without being outrageously costly). For a fine-dining experience (at a dear price), try the Tollbooth Restaurant on the sea front, owned by former owners of Creel Inn.

Day Eight: *Golf on your way to the Fife or wait until you arrive, but today's trip is a pleasant drive down Scotland's east coast.*

Golf: Stonehaven GC is an option if you want to play early in the day. If you want to drive south first, play at Montrose or at Arbroath.
Where to Stay: St. Andrews has plenty of lodging, but they can fill up and be fairly pricey. If St. Andrews lodging doesn't suit you, try one of the several guesthouses in Broughty Ferry near Dundee (the Fisherman's Tavern Hotel is very pleasant).
Where to Eat: In St. Andrews are many of eating choices, including 1 Golf Place or for the more adventurous, drive along the East Neuk Coastal Route to Anstruther and visit the Dreel Tavern.

Day Nine: *Plan time to explore the village of St. Andrews after golf with its shopping, castle, cathedral, and university.*

Golf: Play one of the St. Andrews courses. Plan well in advance if the Old Course is your choice. Otherwise, the Eden Course is right next door.
Where to Stay: Same as day eight.
Where to Eat: The Peat Inn, about six miles east of St. Andrews near Cuper, is a roadside tavern with a tremendous reputation (we just haven't made it there yet).

Day Ten: *Last day of this Scotland adventure.*

Golf: Play one of the Crail courses. As an alternative, drive around the south end of the Fife, and play Lundin Links (we loved it) or Leven Links (we haven't had the chance to try it yet).
Where to Stay: An airport Hotel if you have an early flight out the next day.

TRIP TWO:
THE AYRSHIRE COAST, KINTYRE, AND CENTRAL SCOTLAND

Day One: *Arrive at Glasgow Airport about midday. Pick up your rental car and after a practicing in the parking lot, drive toward Ayr.*

> **Golf:** Play nine holes at Maybole GC or Doon Valley.
> **Where to Stay:** Stay in Alloway at Brig o' Doon House Hotel.
> **Where to Eat:** Brig o' Doon House.

Day Two: *Play golf in the area, and explore some Burns' sites after golf.*

> **Golf:** Play one of the local courses, Belleisle or Seafield.
> **Where to Stay:** Same as day one.
> **Where to Eat:** The Ivy House is a fine restaurant on the grounds of the Belleisle Estate; good food and not too expensive.

Day Three: *Catch the Caledonian MacBrayne Ferry to Isle Arran from Ardrossan, about forty minutes north of Alloway. Ferry schedules are available and tickets can be booked online. Be sure to arrive at the terminal at least a half hour early if you are pre-booked, or an hour early if you don't have reservations. The trip to Brodick on Isle Arran is 55 minutes.*

> **Golf:** We haven't played the Brodick Golf Club (flat links course which tends to be very wet), but we think that either Whiting Bay GC or Lamlash GC will be more interesting.
> **Where to Stay:** The range of accommodations on Isle Arran is broad. For a luxurious stay, try Kilmichael House on the north edge of Brodick. For a more reasonably priced stay, we like The Lily Bank B&B in Lamlash. There are many B&Bs and guesthouse hotels in every village. Use the web to find a place right for you.

Where to Eat: Make the Brodick Bar & Brasserie your spot for a drink and dinner the first night on Arran. The menu is one of the best in Scotland.

Day Four: A day of golf and sightseeing on Isle Arran, Scotland in Miniature. Take the road from Brodick to Blackwaterfoot (B880).

Golf: Play twelve holes at Shiskine Golf and Tennis Club. Then play Shiskine again or, add nine holes at Machrie Bay.
Where to Stay: Same as day three.
Where to Eat: It depends upon which way you head back toward your lodging. If you head north from golf, the Catacol Hotel has quality meals. If you swing south from golf, visit the Lagg Inn . If it's too early for a meal at either of these, drop in for tea or a pint and eat in Brodick, Whiting Bay, or Lamlash.

Day Five: After golf, it's another ferry trip day. Catch the ferry at Lochranza to Claonaig (thirty minute ride) on your way to Campbeltown or Macrihanish.

Golf: Play nine holes at Corrie GC, then later, if you have the time, play nine more at Carradale GC on the Kintyre Peninsula.
Where to Stay: Numerous B&Bs and guesthouses can be found in both Campbeltown and Macrihanish. The one we've stayed at before hasn't responded to messages, so we're afraid to recommend it.
Where to Eat: Ask at your lodging for recommendations.

Day Six: Play a great golf course and take a scenic drive.

Golf: Play eighteen holes at Macrihanish GC—a world-class links track.
Where to Stay: There are two possible destinations for today. First, drive 48 miles north to Lochgilphead, a resort community on Loch Fyne. Staying here would mean a longer drive tomorrow, but one that is along beautiful Loch Lomand. The second option is to drive to Oban, about 35 miles farther north than Lochgilphead. The next day will be about 30 miles shorter, as you head toward Crieff through the Glen of Weeping, Glencoe. Both Oban and Lochgilphead have many lodging options.

Where to Eat: Oban has more options, but ask at your lodging for either. If you stay in Oban, be sure to go to the Oban Inn, at least for a drink.

Day Seven: A drive to Crieff in Central Scotland with golf on the way.

Golf: Play nine or eighteen holes at St. Fillans at the east end of Loch Earn, about 17 miles west of Crieff. If you only play nine at St. Fillans, you may want to play a second nine on the Crieff Dornoch course.
Where to Stay: We suggest a B&B like Merlindale, or a small guesthouse like Arduthie House Hotel.
Where to Eat: Dinner at a local pub (Arduthie, Haggis & Sporan, Meadow Inn).

Day Eight: After golf, stay in the area to explore Drummond Castle Gardens or Famous Grouse Experience (Glenturret Distillery).

Golf: Play eighteen holes at the Crieff Ferntower course.
Where to Stay: Same as day seven.
Where to Eat: If staying at a B&B which serves dinner, like Merlindale, try to arrange a B&B dinner.

Day Nine: Drive the beautiful Sma' Glen to find golf near Aberfeldy.

Golf: Play eighteen holes at the lovely Taymouth Castle course.
Where to Stay: Same as days seven and eight.
Where to Eat: A pub in Crieff or for the adventurous, drive down Glendevon to the Tormaukin Hotel.

Day Ten: The last day of this trip can still be full of Scottish golfing adventure.

Golf: Play eighteen holes at the foot of the castle on Sterling Golf course.
Where to Stay: Stay at an airport hotel if you have an early flight. If you have a later flight, stay again in Crieff (often you can get a discount at a B&B for a stay longer than three days).

TRIP THREE:
EAST LOTHIAN, THE BORDERS, AND THE SOUTH

Day One: *Arrive at Edinburgh about midday. Pick up rental car and take some practice drives around the parking lot. Drive toward East Lothian.*

> **Golf:** Play nine at the Old Musselburgh course (one of the oldest in the world, which plays inside the horse race track) or, if early enough, play eighteen holes at Kilspindie GC.
> **Where to Stay:** Stay in Aberlady at a nice B&B like Aberlady Mains House, or go on to North Berwick, which has many attractive B&Bs or small guesthouse hotels.
> **Where to Eat:** The Old Aberlady Inn is a fine spot for your first evening meal.

Day Two: *Play golf in East Lothians. Try to visit Dirleton Castle, which has a world-renowned garden, or Tantallon Castle, with wonderful views of Bass Rock.*

> **Golf:** Play eighteen on the links of North Berwick West, a British Open qualifying course.
> **Where to Stay:** Same as day one.
> **Where to Eat:** Try another great golfer's pub, The Old Clubhouse in Gullane.

Day Three: *More play in this golf-rich area.*

> **Golf:** Play eighteen holes at one of the Gullane courses, or go farther afield and play eighteen at Dunbar East Links (a Tom Morris 1850 design) in Dunbar near Muirfield. We haven't played any of these courses yet, but they are top-quality venues.
> **Where to Stay:** Same as days one and two.
> **Where to Eat:** Ask for recommendations from your B&B or golf club staff.

Day Four: *Drive into the Borders area and play golf.*

Golf: Play eighteen at Peebles Golf Club.
Where to Stay: There are numerous B&Bs in Peebles. We've always stayed at Lindores House, but the owners have recently sold the B&B. We'd still give it a try because it's a beautiful house with an interesting history.
Where to Eat: We suggest The Traquair Arms Hotel in Innerleithen seven miles east of Peebles for dinner. At Traquair Arms, try the Traquair Jacobite Ale, but be warned: it's over 7% alcohol.

Day Five: *Explore the Borders with Traquair House, its abbeys at Melrose, Dryburgh, and Jedburgh, and play some interesting courses.*

Golf: Start with nine holes at St. Boswell GC near Dryburgh Abbey, then try more golf at Selkirk, Melrose, or Innerleithen.
Where to Stay: Same as day four.
Where to Eat: Try either the Crown Hotel or Neidpath Inn in Peebles.

Day Six: *Last day in the Borders. Play golf and then visit* Abbottsford House or Robert Smail's Print Shop.

Golf: Don't want to drive very far? Play eighteen holes at Cardrona GC (the Border's newest course), about four miles east of Peebles. Up to a bit more of a drive? Play eighteen on Hawick Golf course (the Border's oldest).
Where to Stay: Same as day four and five.
Where to Eat: Drive about five miles toward Edinburgh to the Horseshoe Inn in Eddleston.

Day Seven: *Journey south to explore the southern sites and courses. Stop at Gretna Green, just to say you saw the famous Blacksmith Wedding Chapel.*

Golf: Play eighteen holes on the Solway Firth at the Powfoot Golf Club.
Where to Stay: Stay at the Powfoot Golf Hotel next to the course. When you book lodging, be sure to ask about stay-and-play deals.

Where to Eat: The Powfoot Golf Hotel is well respected for its pub meals.

Day Eight: Visit the Dumfries area and play the best-known of the southern courses. We suggest skipping the town of Dumfries to leave time to visit Sweetheart Abbey and New Abbey Corn Mill.

Golf: Play eighteen holes at Southerness Golf course (31 miles east and south from Powfoot, 16 miles south of Dumfries).
Where to Stay: Stay again at Powfoot Golf Hotel or, if you want more time to explore the south's largest town of Dumfries, book a B&B or guesthouse hotel in town.
Where to Eat: Depending upon where you are staying, ask for recommendations.

Day Nine: It's a sixty-mile drive (mostly freeway or very good road) up to West Linton, heading back toward your flight home.

Golf: Play eighteen holes on West Linton GC's moorland track.
Where to Stay: The Golden Arms Hotel in West Linton is about the only place to stay.
Where to Eat: The Golden Arms serves very tasty meals.

Day Ten: Last day to play in Scotland.

Golf: We love West Linton GC so much that we'd probably play it again, but if you want a different course, try Rutherford Castle GC in West Linton, or Carnwath GC, about 14 miles southwest of West Linton. We haven't played either of these courses, but have looked at Carnwath and think it would be fun to play.
Where to Stay: Stay at an airport hotel, if you have an early flight. Otherwise, stay again in West Linton, only 12 miles from Edinburgh airport.

OWER AT LAST

Our lists are done, but yours should just be getting started. Pour over the maps and guide books. You know you'll want to see Glasgow and Edinburgh. You'll probably want to play the Old Course and Turnberry or Carnoustie. To make your trip complete start a list of the other courses you may wish to play: Crieff, Crail, Fortrose, Reay. Make a list also of the other sights to see: Blair Atholl, Clava Cairns, Melrose Abbey.

Your hidden gem Scotland adventure awaits.
Slainte Mhor!

Index

A

Abbottsford House, 128, 190
Aberlady Mains House B&B, 189
Abernethy Round Tower, 100, 106
Alloway Kirk yard, 164
Anstruther GC, 13, 93, 109
Arduaine Gardens, 166
Arduthie House Hotel, 38-9, 188
Arran Aromatics, 165, 172, 181
Auld Brig o' Doon, 158
Auchagallon stone Circle, 165
Auchterarder GC, 31-2, 46
Auchterlonie, Willie, 27, 149
Aviemore, 67

B

Bad Ass Bistro, 6
Balbirnie GC, 96, 103, 110
Balhousie Castle, 26, 42-3
Balmerino Abbey, 106-7
Baxter's Highland Village, 88
Belleisle GC, 145-6, 168, 186
Ben Lawers Mountain Visitor Centre, 29
Benromach Distillery, 87
Black Isle, 53
Bladnoch Distillery, 136
Bladnoch Inn, 136
Blair Atholl GC, 50-1, 70
Blair Castle, 61, 68-9
Boat of Garten GC, 13, 15, 52, 58, 71, 174-5, 179, 182
Booktown, (Wigtown), 142
Braid, James, 29, 33, 52-3, 57-8, 62, 74, 92, 113, 132, 146
Bramberger, Michael, 152
Brig o' Doon House Hotel, 158, 177, 186
British Golf Museum, 167
Brodick Bar & Brasserie, 159, 177, 187

Brodick Castle, 165
Brodick GC, 148, 186
Brora GC, 57, 61, 72
buggies, 10-11, 28, 95, 149
bump and run, 14
Bunillidh Restaurant, 66-7, 177
Burns Cottage, 164
Burns Monument, 164
Burns Statue, 138
Burntisland GC,95-6, 101, 110
Byre Bistro, 17, 29, 41-2

C

caddy carts, 50
Caerlaverock Castle, 137, 141
Cairn Holy Chambered Cairns, 139, 142
Cairngorm Railway, 59
Caithness Glass, 26, 42
Caledonian MacBrayne Ferries, 148, 164, 186
Catacol Hotel, 160-1, 187
Cardoness Castle, 142
Cardrona GC, 115, 121, 130, 190
Carnwath GC, 191
Carradale GC, 151-2, 157, 169, 187
Castle Kennedy Gardens, 140, 142
Castle Trail, 75, 80, 87
Cawdor Castle, 69
Clava Cairns, 69
clifftop, 12
Clootie Dumpling, 65
Coasters, 156, 161
Colt, Harry S., 97, 112
Comrie GC, 27, 45
Corner House Hotel, 118
Corrie GC, 11, 148, 154, 168, 187
Cotton, Henry 38
Craigievar Castle, 184
Crail Balcombie GC, 94, 109, 173

Crail Craighead GC, 94-5, 103, 109
credit cards, 22-3
Creel Inn, 79, 177, 185
Crieff Dornoch GC, 6, 26, 45, 179, 188
Crieff Ferntower GC, 6, 26-7, 34, 45, 179, 188
Crieff Hotel, 39
Crossraguel Abbey, 163-4
Crown Hotel, 119, 190
Crows Nest Pub, 65
Cullen GC, 76, 89
cullen skink, 65, 76, 81
Culloden, 69-70
Culzean Castle, 153, 163

D

Dalmally GC, 153, 169
Dalwhinnie Distillery, 68
Dawyck Gardens, 126-7
Dewer's World of Whisky, 36, 44
Dirleton Castle, 189
dogs, 4, 17, 19, 62, 66, 114, 118, 124
Doonbrae B&B, 158
Doon Valley GC, 147-8, 168, 186
Dornoch Struie GC, 56, 184
Dreel Tavern, 99, 177, 183, 185
drinking water, 10, 16-7
Drouthy Neebors, 99, 104
Drummond Castle Gardens, 26, 35, 43, 179
Dryburgh Abbey, 126
Duart Castle, 167
Duff House, 88
Dufftown GC, 75, 89
Dumfries, 137
Dunadd, 166
Dunbar East Links GC, 189
Dundarave House B&B, 179
Dunfermline Cathedral & Palace, 106

Dunfermline Pitfirrane GC, 96-7, 110
Dunnottar Castle, 74, 86
Dunollie Castle, 167
Dunrobin Castle, 69
Dunstaffnage Castle, 166

E

Eagle Hotel, 65-6, 177, 184
Easter Aquhorthie Stone Circle, 86
East Neuk, 93, 185
Edradour Distillery, 64, 68, 179
Eilein Castle, 59
Elgin GC, 78, 90

F

Fortrose & Rosemarkie GC, 7, 53-4, 71, 174-5, 177, 184
Famous Grouse Experience, 43-4, 179
Fisherman's Tavern Hotel, 185
Fernie, Willie, 50, 149, 150
Frommer's Road Atlas Britain, 10
Fyvie Castle, 82, 88
Fyvie Parish Kirk, 88

G

Gillespie, Curtis, 125
Girvan GC, 134-5, 143
Glencorse GC, 116, 130
Gleneagles Resort, 31, 115
Glen Grant Distillery, 87
Glenmorangie Distillery, 68, 184
Glenturret Distillery, 43-4, 179
Golden Arms, 4, 7, 19, 124, 191
Gordon Arms Hotel, 80
Golf Courses in Scotland (map), 10
Golf Tavern, 6
Golspie GC, 57, 72
gorse, 13

Grantown-on-Spey GC, 52-3, 58, 71
Gretna Green, 190
gun platform green, 148

H

Haggis & Sporan, 39-40
handicap, 13-4, 55
Hanse, Gil, 94
Hawick GC,117, 130, 190
heathland, 12
Helmsdale GC, 57, 62, 72
Highland Laddie Pub, 136-7
hilly, 11
Historic Scotland, 22, 88, 137
honesty box, 12, 18, 54
honors, 13
Hope & Anchor Pub, 136
Hopeman GC, 78, 82, 85, 90, 184
Horseshoe Inn, 124-5, 190
Huntingdon Hotel, 136
Huntingtower Castle, 35, 42
Huntly Castle, 87-8

I

inland, 12
Innerleithen GC, 12, 112, 129
Innerpeffray Library & Chapel, 26, 37, 44-5
Iona Abbey, 167
Iona Nunnery, 167
Island Cheese Co., 165, 172, 181
Ivy House, The, 186

J

James Braid Golfing Society, 57
Jedburgh Abbey, 121, 126
Johnnie Fox Irish Pub, 64

K

Kailzie Gardens, 127
Keg Lounge, 119
Kenmore GC, 29, 46
Killin GC, 28-9, 45, 177

Killin Hotel & Riverside Bistro, 40-1
Kilmichael House, 186
Kilspindie GC, 116, 130, 189
Kimberley Inn, 81, 86
Kinghorn GC, 95, 109
Kings Arms, 136
Kingsbarns GC, 95
King's Cave, 150
King James VI GC, 32, 47
Kingussie GC, 51-2, 70
Kinneuchar Inn, 99
Kirkcudbright, 137

L

Lagg Inn, 160, 187
Lamlash GC, 149, 155, 168, 186
Leven GC, 92, 185
Lilybank House B&B, 171, 186
Lindores House B&B, 113, 118, 190
linksland, 12
Lochleven Castle, 105-6
Lochranza Distillery, 160, 172
Loch Tummel Inn, 64-5, 177
Lock Inn, 3
Lundin Ladies GC, 92-3, 102, 109
Lundin Links GC, 92, 109

M

MacDonald Cardrona Hotel Golf & Country Club, 115
MacGrochen's Bar, 161
Machrie Bay GC, 151, 169, 172, 180
Machrie Moor, 165
Macrihanish GC, 13, 152-3, 156, 169, 174, 187
Made in Scotland Shop, 67-8
Mallin House Hotel, 66, 184
Maybole GC, 147, 168, 186
McCraig's Tower or Folly, 166
McLean's Real Music Bar, 63
Meadow Inn, 39
Melrose Abbey, 122, 126

Merlindale B&B, 4, 179, 188
meters, convert to yards, 11
Middleton, Fraser, 96
Monarch of the Glen, 51
moorland, 12
Morris, Old Tom, 26, 32, 55,
    76, 93-4, 101, 107, 108,
    152, 189
Morris, Young Tom, 38, 101,
    108
Moss Farm Stone Circle, 165
Moulin Hotel & Inn, 64, 177,
    179, 181
Muckart GC, 32, 46
Murrayshall GC, 33, 36, 47,
    174
Murrayshall Lynedoch GC,
    33, 47
Museum of Ancient Culture,
    166
Muthill GC, 31, 46
Myrtle Inn, 6

N

Nairn Dunbar GC, 78-9, 90,
    184
Nairn GC, 78
National Trust for Scotland,
    22, 29, 106-7, 129, 163
Neidpath Inn, 119, 124, 190
Nether Largie Stone Circle,
    155
New Abbey Corn Mill, 137,
    191
North Berwick West GC, 13,
    116-17, 122-3, 130, 174,
    176, 189

O

1 Golf Place, 104, 185
Oban Distillery, 166
Oban Inn, 162, 188
*Official Guide to Golf in
    Scotland*, 10, 22
Old Aberlady Inn, 125, 177,
    189
Old Bridge Inn, 65
Old Clubhouse, 125, 189
Old Course, St. Andrews, 91,
    97, 113, 185
Old Musselburgh GC, 189
Oran's Chapel, 167

P

packing, 15
Pantry, The, 159-60, 173
Park Hotel & Bar, 119
parking, 20
parkland, 12
Park, Jr., Willie, 95, 114, 150
Peat Inn, The, 185
Peebles GC, 112-3, 120,
    129, 190
Piershead Tavern, 159
Pitlochry, 60, 63, 179
Pitlochry GC, 10, 49-50, 67,
    70
power carts, 10-11, 149
Powfoot GC, 132, 138-9,
    143, 190
Powfoot Golf Hotel, 132,
    135, 190-1
price of golf, 12-13, 75
pull carts, 11, 50

Q

Queen Victoria, 29, 40, 161
Queen's View, 65

R

Reay GC, 62, 72,
Road Atlas Britain, 10
Robert Smail's Print Shop,
    123, 128-9, 190
Ross, Donald, 55
Rosslyn Chapel, 128
Ross, MacKenzie, 132
Roundwood GC, Ireland, 149
Royal Arch Lounge, 104-5
Royal Dornoch GC, 13, 55-6,
    60, 71, 175, 177, 182, 184
Royal Hotel, Comrie, 40
Royal Hotel, Kirkcudbright,
    136
Royal Tarlair GC, 75-6, 85,
    89
Rubenstein, Lorne, 55
Rutherford Castle GC, 191

S

Sayers, Ben, 77, 117
Scone Palace, 43

*Scotland's A-Z Visitor's
    Atlas*, 10
Scotland's Secret Bunker,
    107
Seafield GC, 146-7, 168, 186
Seafield Arms Hotel &
    Lounge, 81, 84
seaside, 12
Ship Inn, 124
Ship Tavern, 98-9, 102
Shiskine Golf & Tennis Club,
    150-1, 169, 172, 175-6,
    183, 187
Silloth on Solway GC, 13,
    133, 140, 143, 173
single track roads, 21, 151
Souter Johnnie's Cottage,
    164
Southerness GC, 132-3,
    143, 191
speed of play, 13-14
Spey Bay GC, 77-8, 90
Speyside Cooperage, 83, 87
Speyside Heather Garden,
    65
St. Andrews Castle &
    Cathedral, 100, 107-8
St. Andrews Eden Course,
    97-8, 110, 185
St. Andrews Links Trust,
    97-8
St. Andrews Old Course, 91,
    97, 113, 185
St. Andrews Strathtyrum
    Course, 98, 110
St. Andrews University, 107
St. Boswell GC, 114-5, 130,
    190
St. Columba, 167
St. Fillan, 28, 162
St. Fillans GC, 6, 11, 18,
    26-7, 45, 174, 177, 188
St. Medans GC, 134, 141,
    143
St. Rule's Church, 108
Steel, Donald, 98
Sterling Castle, 37, 43
Sterling GC, 37-8, 47, 188
Stonehaven GC, 73, 83, 89,
    185
stovies, 63
Strathlene Buckie GC, 77, 89

Strathspey Steam Railroad, 52, 67
Strathtay GC, 30-1, 46
Stuart Glass, 26, 42
Stutt, Hamilton, 33
Stutt, J.R., 96
Suie Lodge, 157, 162
Sutherland House, 66, 184
Sweetheart Abbey, 137, 191

Whiting Bay GC, 11, 149-50, 169, 186
Wigtown & Bladnoch GC, 133-4, 143
Wigtown Martyr's Monument, 134
Wildings Hotel, 158
Williamson, Colonel, 27

XYZ

yardage markers, 11

T

Tain GC, 54-5, 71, 176, 184
Tam o' Shanter Pub, 147
Tantallon Castle, 189
Tarbat GC, 12, 54, 71
Taymouth Castle GC, 29-30, 46, 188
Thomas, Dave, 115
Threave Castle, 137, 142
Three Kings Inn, 80-1, 84
tipping, 17, 20
toilets, 10, 27, 113
Tollbooth Restaurant, 185
Tormaukin Hotel, 32, 41, 177, 188
Torphins GC, 75, 89
Torrylin Cairn,160, 165
Tourist Information Bureau (The I), 3-4, 10, 22
Traquair Arms Hotel, 118-9, 177, 190
Traquair House, 120, 127-8, 159
trolleys, 11, 50, 95, 114, 147
two-for-one schemes, 14

UVW

uisge beatha, 17, 86
undulating, 11
vacation golf, 15, 76
Vardon, Harry, 51
Victory gardens, 92, 132
Water of Life, 17, 68, 86
Weaver's Bar, 104
West Linton GC, 4, 10, 113-4, 129, 191
whins, 13
whisky, 17, 39, 86-7
Whisky Trail, 68, 75, 80, 86